Universities and Colleges: A Very Short Introduction

VERY SHORT INTRODUCTIONS are for anyone wanting a stimulating and accessible way into a new subject. They are written by experts, and have been translated into more than 45 different languages.

The series began in 1995, and now covers a wide variety of topics in every discipline. The VSI library currently contains over 500 volumes—a Very Short Introduction to everything from Psychology and Philosophy of Science to American History and Relativity—and continues to grow in every subject area.

Very Short Introductions available now:

ACCOUNTING Christopher Nobes
ADOLESCENCE Peter K. Smith
ADVERTISING Winston Fletcher
AFRICAN AMERICAN RELIGION
    Eddie S. Glaude Jr
AFRICAN HISTORY John Parker and
    Richard Rathbone
AFRICAN RELIGIONS Jacob K. Olupona
AGEING Nancy A. Pachana
AGNOSTICISM Robin Le Poidevin
AGRICULTURE Paul Brassley and
    Richard Soffe
ALEXANDER THE GREAT
    Hugh Bowden
ALGEBRA Peter M. Higgins
AMERICAN HISTORY Paul S. Boyer
AMERICAN IMMIGRATION
    David A. Gerber
AMERICAN LEGAL HISTORY
    G. Edward White
AMERICAN POLITICAL HISTORY
    Donald Critchlow
AMERICAN POLITICAL PARTIES
    AND ELECTIONS L. Sandy Maisel
AMERICAN POLITICS
    Richard M. Valelly
THE AMERICAN PRESIDENCY
    Charles O. Jones
THE AMERICAN REVOLUTION
    Robert J. Allison
AMERICAN SLAVERY
    Heather Andrea Williams
THE AMERICAN WEST Stephen Aron
AMERICAN WOMEN'S HISTORY
    Susan Ware

ANAESTHESIA Aidan O'Donnell
ANALYTIC PHILOSOPHY
    Michael Beaney
ANARCHISM Colin Ward
ANCIENT ASSYRIA Karen Radner
ANCIENT EGYPT Ian Shaw
ANCIENT EGYPTIAN ART AND
    ARCHITECTURE Christina Riggs
ANCIENT GREECE Paul Cartledge
THE ANCIENT NEAR EAST
    Amanda H. Podany
ANCIENT PHILOSOPHY Julia Annas
ANCIENT WARFARE Harry Sidebottom
ANGELS David Albert Jones
ANGLICANISM Mark Chapman
THE ANGLO-SAXON AGE John Blair
ANIMAL BEHAVIOUR
    Tristram D. Wyatt
THE ANIMAL KINGDOM
    Peter Holland
ANIMAL RIGHTS David DeGrazia
THE ANTARCTIC Klaus Dodds
ANTISEMITISM Steven Beller
ANXIETY Daniel Freeman and
    Jason Freeman
THE APOCRYPHAL GOSPELS
    Paul Foster
ARCHAEOLOGY Paul Bahn
ARCHITECTURE Andrew Ballantyne
ARISTOCRACY William Doyle
ARISTOTLE Jonathan Barnes
ART HISTORY Dana Arnold
ART THEORY Cynthia Freeland
ASIAN AMERICAN HISTORY
    Madeline Y. Hsu

Available soon:

For more information visit our website

www.oup.com/vsi/

David Palfreyman and Paul Temple

UNIVERSITIES AND COLLEGES

A Very Short Introduction

OXFORD
UNIVERSITY PRESS

OXFORD
UNIVERSITY PRESS

Great Clarendon Street, Oxford, OX2 6DP,
United Kingdom

Oxford University Press is a department of the University of Oxford.
It furthers the University's objective of excellence in research, scholarship,
and education by publishing worldwide. Oxford is a registered trade mark of
Oxford University Press in the UK and in certain other countries

© David Palfreyman and Paul Temple 2017

The moral rights of the authors have been asserted

First edition published 2017

Published in the United States of America by Oxford University Press
198 Madison Avenue, New York, NY 10016, United States of America

British Library Cataloguing in Publication Data
Data available

Library of Congress Control Number: 2017947628

ISBN 978-0-19-876613-1

Printed and bound by
CPI Group (UK) Ltd, Croydon, CR0 4YY

To the Memory of Professor Sir David Watson (1949–2015), sometime Vice-Chancellor of Brighton University and latterly Principal of Green-Templeton College Oxford—a scholar, a wise leader in higher education, and a perceptive thinker about the university; and who commented in his last book: 'To attempt to capture a holistic view of the modern university is a foolhardy goal'.

Contents

Preface

One of the several difficulties of writing a 'very short introduction' to universities and colleges is not simply the breadth of the topic that has to be fitted into a short book, but that it consists of various strands which are tightly interwoven and which we have to tease out. Most studies of universities and colleges examine just one or two of these strands in depth: we need to look, if only briefly, at most if not all of them, and try to show the connections between them. We hope that we have managed to do this while not allowing detailed explanations to obscure the wider landscape that we are trying to map. For convenience, from now on when we refer to 'universities' we also include 'colleges' in which higher education, leading to the award of degrees, is taking place.

Universities have been around in Europe in something vaguely resembling their present form for 900 years, so a historical dimension is inevitable. They now exist in recognizable forms (though with important local variations) in nearly all countries of the world, so an international dimension is necessary. They undertake a range of tasks that at first sight don't have obvious connections, and they typically have unusual internal arrangements—so a functional analysis is required. How they are financed (how much, paid by whom) varies considerably, and is often a matter of controversy: these are key issues in 'the politics of higher education'. They perform roles related to the social structures of the societies in which they are located, and now, in most countries, they are seen as essential drivers of economic growth—so there are sociological, political, and economic aspects to understand.

All these various strands—historical, international, functional, financial, sociological, political, economic—interact with one another. Long-established universities are often seen as being more prestigious than newer ones, and more likely to play a role in the formation of national elites. Universities with significant research functions may be seen as crucial for national economic development, receiving public and private financial support as a result. Universities may be given regional development remits but at the same time be expected to operate internationally. Many countries have universities that are publicly controlled as well as others that are private. These characteristics can produce curiously contradictory expectations of universities—more so, perhaps, than for almost any other organizational form. They are generally expected to be simultaneously traditional yet innovative; elite yet open; competitive yet collegial; international yet local; and so on. Universities often try to resolve these contradictions in different ways, which explains why superficially similar institutions have, on further examination, developed quite different organizational cultures. It is not surprising that people outside the world of higher education find universities baffling.

This book has the word 'universities' in its title. There is a broader area of post-school study, sometimes called 'higher' or 'tertiary education', which includes universities but also a range of other institutions and levels of study—this is sometimes described as 'ISCED Level 5', a reference to the UNESCO International Standard Classification of Education. Some of these institutions may have specific professional or technical orientations, while others may be general in scope. There is no hard-and-fast distinction between what in one country may be called a university and in another, a college: in Britain, it would have been reasonable just a few years ago to say that universities could be distinguished from other tertiary institutions by virtue of their undertaking research, but this is no longer the case. The important point is to understand how a country's tertiary education institutions in total relate to its school system, to its economy and society, and to one another. Comparative education studies show that what apparently works well in one country may not work at all in another.

Universities and other tertiary institutions have, over the last few decades, come to be considered, both by national governments and international agencies, as key elements in what has become known as the 'knowledge economy' (or, more grandly, the 'knowledge society'). This was an unknown concept when the two authors were themselves students (which is not to say that getting a good job was not, then as now, a central motivation for going to university; getting away from home was another) but it is now a commonplace. From the point of view of universities, it is of course convenient to be seen as having this key role when it comes to their extracting money from governments and students; but it also means that governments may decide to involve themselves in the operation of universities to a greater extent than in even the recent past, when universities were typically seen as being rather marginal to whatever governments saw as the pressing needs of society and managing the economy. The close interest of governments, in many countries, in their local universities has been a big, historically sudden, and important change. So the tension between universities believing that they are best placed to run their own affairs—a sense that is deeply rooted in most academic cultures—and governments demanding a say in what they are doing, sometimes with matters of national pride involved, is one that is, we suspect, becoming more acute in many countries.

We end this book with a short chapter on the future university. One theme in literature on higher education emphasizes the longevity and adaptability of the university as an organizational form, while another theme predicts its demise (globalization and the Internet being the current villains of the piece). Other critiques suggest that while something called 'the university' will continue to exist, it will have lost its central intellectual purpose. We are, broadly, optimists on the future of the university, even though the idea of 'the university' now makes little sense—there will be multiple, overlapping ideas of the university, reflecting the growing significance and variability of knowledge production and its dissemination throughout all modern societies. We hope that the picture this book paints will provide a context for understanding these changes.

The Further Reading section will enable readers to follow up on the many themes, topics, and trends concerning higher education and the management of universities that we have introduced in this short book.

We should be frank about one particular difficulty with which we have struggled. As we have just noted, universities are peculiar in having spread right across the globe while maintaining certain basic functional similarities and even many common processes. But at the same time, creating a useful taxonomy of universities even for a single country is difficult because, on close study, a wide range of variations to the basic pattern emerges. We naturally know some higher education systems better than others, and it is, we are afraid, therefore inevitable that our descriptions will be coloured by this knowledge. As such, we focus on the UK and the US, less so on Europe and much less so on Asia, Latin America, Africa, or Oceania. We can only apologize to readers from countries who feel—no doubt, correctly—that their own higher education tradition has been poorly served by us.

The authors are grateful to colleagues who have very kindly read through our draft text and made many helpful comments—Professor Dennis Ahlberg, John Edmunds, Professor Ian McNay, and Professor David Warner—but errors and omissions remain solely the responsibility of the authors.

A note on 'colleges'

As we have already stressed, in this book, when we use the terms 'university' or 'universities' we also mean the 'college' or 'colleges' in which higher education takes place and students work towards earning a degree. Estimates vary wildly, but there are at least some 17,000 such 'higher education institutions' globally, with more than 150 million students. We are not able in this very short book to cover in addition the important task that many of these colleges undertake in providing vocational courses by way of further or tertiary education following on from the end of compulsory school attendance. These courses also take place in the very many colleges not involved with delivering higher education, and they lead to qualification as, say, a plumber, hair stylist, electrician, beautician, or car mechanic. Such courses are taught across, for example, the vast network of community colleges in the US or in the further education colleges within the UK, as well as in the *technische Hochschule* and polytechnic institutions in such nations as Germany and the Netherlands. But, at least in the US and UK, as we have noted, higher education may also be taking place in many of these same colleges.

Historically, a 'college' might have included the likes of the medieval College of the Sorbonne that became part of the University of Paris, or one of the many constituent colleges within the federal University of Oxford or Cambridge—and these still exist. Similarly, a 'college' might refer to one of the constituent parts of the University of London, such as Imperial College or King's College, that are now in effect independent and sizeable universities but still retain the word 'college' in their titles. A 'college' is used in the US to refer to a liberal arts college, such as Dartmouth College, which in many countries would be labelled a 'university'; and undergraduates today attending Harvard University are still placed within its 'Harvard College'. Thus, in America students 'go to college' (even if attending a large state university campus) while the young British student 'goes to uni' (even if a few of these in fact attend a college at Oxbridge, or go to Imperial, UCL, and King's in London—and, in pre-war decades, the English undergraduate might have been said to 'go to the varsity'!).

Almost all of the wide range of themes and issues we address in this little book to do with the governance, management, funding, student recruitment, teaching quality, and degree standards of a university or universities will apply equally to any college or colleges in which similar higher education is being delivered. And, indeed, many of these same themes and issues, problems and challenges apply just as much to the management of the further and vocational education being offered in, say, the US community colleges or the UK further education colleges. Perhaps, however, a significant difference is that research is much less likely to be happening in 'colleges', just as, in practice, it does not take place in all 'universities'. We are sorry if this idea of 'universities and colleges' is beginning to sound a tad complicated, but in this Very Short Introduction we are trying to explore both the university and college as a concept, and universities and colleges as actual institutions that have evolved over about 1,000 years from their origins in medieval Europe and have now spread globally as part of the tertiary post-school life experience of a growing proportion of the world's population. We begin at the beginning, in 12th-century Europe...

List of illustrations

Chapter 1
The enduring idea and changing ideal of the university

Versions of 'the university' existed in Greece and China some 2,500 years ago and the concept of a centre of higher learning survived in Arab countries during the so-called Dark Ages of 500–1000 CE across Europe. But the model for the modern university began its long evolution from its creation about 1,000 years ago in medieval Western Europe. This is the enduring idea of the university that we explore in this Very Short Introduction: an idea that adjusts and adapts as a changing ideal form over the centuries.

The derivation of the word 'university' is from the Latin, *universitas*, meaning 'the whole'; and the earliest recorded usage is from 1300. This idea of 'the whole' will recur throughout this book—it might refer to 'the whole body of teachers and students pursuing, at a particular place, the higher branches of learning' (as the *Oxford English Dictionary* definition puts it); or it might refer to the idea that knowledge, the business of universities, is, ultimately, indivisible—a whole. The closely associated term 'college' is derived from the Latin *collegium*, meaning an association or corporation, and the earliest use given is in the 1379 legal documentation for the creation of New College, University of Oxford. We shall see that the notion of an association or a guild of scholars is at the heart of what universities do and how they are organized.

In the US, the two words 'university' and 'college' are often used interchangeably, where typically the student 'goes to college'—whether to a massive State university campus or to a small liberal arts college. In other places, a student may be attending a college within the federal structures of perhaps Cambridge University or London University; or be studying at one of the autonomous faculties of the Sorbonne University in Paris; or be within an 'honours college' set up inside a large US university. In the expanding and diversifying world of higher education, exploring university titles and structures requires some understanding of how the higher education system in question works, and why it is the way it is. We hope this book will help.

There are more students than ever before: over 150 million in over 17,000 institutions around the world, and this number is growing all the time—with over thirty million students in China; some thirty million in India; more than twenty million in over 4,000 universities and colleges within the US; and more than two million across 150 or so institutions in the UK. In the US, about 70 per cent of high-school leavers progress into some form of higher education, as do nearly 50 per cent in the UK, although graduation rates (the proportion of students entering higher education who leave with a degree) are higher in the UK. Moreover, as we will explore later, an increasing number of students are not 'at a particular place', as the *OED* definition had it: they are distance-learning students, linked digitally to a university that itself may have few, or no, students physically present; or, in the US, they may move from one campus to another, picking up credits towards a degree.

For most people (including university staff and students), however, the university is to a large extent about a physical presence, with a vision of an architectural style that includes quadrangles and clock-towers coming into many people's minds. It may no longer so centrally include a library, when students can now access so much material online; yet, historically, the university has been a repository of knowledge powerfully symbolized by its library. But in the past century and a half, the role of research—the creation of new knowledge—has become a co-equal aspect with the preservation and transmission of knowledge, if not in fact now the prime element in the strategic mission of what are regarded as 'leading' universities around the world. This search for prestige or brand status, over the past decade increasingly defined by positions in so-called university ranking tables, is a powerful, arguably distorting, factor in managing such universities and also for other universities that seek to emulate what may be seen as the global leaders.

The university and college as we see them all around the globe today are, essentially, creations from medieval Europe, as much a permanent legacy by way of institutions as the great cathedrals are physically—although some buildings in Oxford and Cambridge also originate from the Middle Ages (see Figure 1). There had, however, been centres of learning and teaching before this, such as Plato's Academy near Athens during the 380s BCE, whose pupil, Aristotle, in turn founded a school known as the Lyceum. There had also been extensive libraries—the Library of Alexandria in Egypt, for instance, was created in the 3rd century BCE but faded away by about 400 CE; it contained perhaps half a million books (as, initially, papyrus scrolls) and preserved the classical learning of academics such as Aristotle and Plato. The Library of Alexandria was part of the *Musaeum* of Alexandria, which resembled a modern university campus since it included lecture theatres, meeting rooms, and dining areas. Later, ancient Greek and Islamic scholarship—gathered in the 'translation movement' and preserved in such centres as the 9th-century Baghdad Academy of Sciences and the University of al-Qarawiyyin in Morocco (dating from 859 BCE and perhaps the oldest, continually operating, degree-issuing institution of higher education in the world)—developed this learning which was subsequently conveyed by scholars in the first universities of Western Europe.

1. New College, Oxford—the 1380s Great Quadrangle, prototype of many since the Oxford quadrangle ('court' in Cambridge) became the iconic symbol of university architecture (later often combined with a clock-tower; see Figure 3).

In Baghdad for some 400 years the Bayt al-Hikma (the House of Wisdom) echoed the Library and Musaeum of Alexandria, not only preserving the ancient Greek learning but adding to it. There were other ancient institutions of higher learning around the world: for example, major Buddhist monasteries in India such as at Nalanda (for some 700 years up to around 1200 CE and perhaps peaking at 10,000 students) and at Taxila (for probably 1,000 years or so until the 5th century CE); and also in ancient China there was an imperial academy, the Taixue, in Peking/Beijing from the 3rd century CE. Overlapping with the creation of the Western university model (as the focus of this book) we find similar libraries and centres of Islamic higher learning in, for instance, Timbuktu (West Africa)—which thrived from the 13th century CE for some 400 years, with fifty or more libraries across the modern city of Timbuktu still containing over half a million manuscripts.

Independently of ancient Greek learning, sophisticated mathematics also evolved in ancient China—there being, for example, a maths textbook from about 200 BCE that used algebraic methods not (re-)invented in the West until almost 2,000 years later, while other methods were in use in China some 300 years before being separately discovered by Newton. Similarly, in India the nine-number (1–9) system emerged by about 300 CE and later came the use of 0 as another number. All this important learning from the East, along with that of ancient Greece as already noted, fed into the newly created European universities of the 12th and 13th centuries via the medieval centres of Islamic learning—giving us, say, the Hindu-Arabic numeral system (0–9) and the basis of modern algebra, plus the decimal point. This knowledge and these ideas, and also inventions, flowed to the West along the Silk Road from China and India, just as did spices and silk. Along the way there was a mingling with the learning of Arab scholars and philosophers such as Avicenna in 11th-century Persia, and on reaching the early European universities this flow of higher learning and of the 'lost' texts of antiquity was enthusiastically taken up by such 13th-century scholars as Roger Bacon, who moved between Oxford and Paris.

Thus, 'the 12th-century renaissance' saw the emergence of universities at Bologna, Paris, Oxford, and Cambridge (Box 1): an evolution drawing, as we have stressed, on the earlier Hellenistic learning which 'the Golden Age of Islam' (8th to the 13th centuries CE) had not only sustained but also added to during 'the Dark Ages' across Western Europe following the collapse of the Roman Empire in the 5th century CE. In the 12th-century scholars such as Adelard of Bath and later Daniel of Morley travelled far searching for 'the studies of the Arabs' and duly brought back to England what the latter termed 'the learning of the Arabs' in the form of 'a precious multitude of books'.

The reasons for these roaming scholars—such as Abelard of Paris, John of Salisbury, Robert Grosseteste, and William of Ockham—to

Box 1. On the spread of universities across medieval Europe

Selected universities from the fifty or so founded before 1500, and besides the oldest surviving four of Bologna (1088), Paris (1150), Oxford (1167), and Cambridge (1209), showing the spread of higher education across Europe. In some cases town v. gown violence forced scholars to flee and to establish a new *universitas* or teaching guild elsewhere: for instance, from Oxford to Cambridge in 1209 and from Paris to Orleans in 1227; the 1355 St Scholastica's Day riots involved dozens of deaths, but the Oxford scholars did not retreat on this occasion. And, over the centuries, some universities were short-lived, declining and fading away, or they were suddenly closed down by a vengeful bishop or monarch and also lost to history (e.g. Alcala, Bourges, Buda, and Wittenberg); while others, medieval collectives of scholars or 'schools', simply did not quite make it to 'universitas' status (e.g. Northampton and Stamford in England).

Bologna	1088
Paris	1150
Oxford	1167
Cambridge	1209
Padua	1222
Toulouse	1229
Salamanca	1255
Lisbon	1290
Prague	1347
Krakow	1364
Vienna	1365
Heidelberg	1385
St Andrews	1410
Rostock	1419
Louvain	1425
Catania	1444
Basle	1459
Copenhagen	1476
Uppsala	1477

end up collected together in such far-flung places might be to do with gaining protection from government, the geography of river-crossing points, or some other rather random factor. These academics organized themselves along the lines of the guilds that dominated crafts and trade, and formed a *universitas* (a collective) of teaching Masters, which would elect its head; be able to own property; and operate as a *studium generale*, teaching and examining students as apprentices—with Latin used as the medium for lectures and scholarly discourse. The core curriculum comprised the seven liberal arts—the *trivium* of grammar, rhetoric, and logic; and the *quadrivium* of arithmetic, geometry, music, and astronomy. The first level degree was the Bachelor of Arts (BA), earned by undergraduates over four years (although at Cambridge in the 1450s, duly responding to the market, the student could pay higher fees to study over the summer and thereby reduce the time to three years). The Master of Arts (MA) took another four years and earned the Master the right to teach at any other university in Christian Europe (*ius ubique docendi*)—today's Master's is usually a one- or two-year degree. Then, for some students, another six to ten years of study culminated in a Doctorate in law, medicine, or theology (the equivalent of today's PhD): the first two, even back in the Middle Ages, being nicknamed 'the lucrative sciences'; the last, being rather less well-rewarded in this world, was at least styled 'the queen of sciences'.

In due course, within these fledgling universities, colleges were founded by wealthy and powerful benefactors as charitable corporations, being awarded a royal charter by the monarch as a means of recognition and of signalling his or her protection: for instance, La Sorbonne (1257) at Paris; Balliol (1263) or Merton (1264) at Oxford; along with Peterhouse (1284) at Cambridge (Figure 2). Oxford and Cambridge Universities are unusual in that their colleges have survived as independent, and in some cases also well-endowed, legal entities—although they did come close to being abolished in the 1530s English Reformation as were the Catholic monasteries and chantries, but fortunately for them

2. Chaundler Manuscript, 1460s, representing New College, Oxford—the idealized concept of the medieval academic guild.

King Henry VIII declared: 'I judge no land in England better bestowed than that which is given to our universities, for by their maintenance our realm shall be well governed when we be dead and rotten.' Indeed, the colleges collectively in each university are richer than the university itself—Trinity College, Cambridge, being the wealthiest with an endowment of some £1 billion. Like any guild, the Masters sought to defend their privileges and eliminate competition—Oxford and Cambridge, for example, enhancing their monopoly by urging the King to suppress incipient universities at Northampton and later at Stamford. The students of the medieval universities were divided into 'nations', and tales of their rowdy, drunken antics survive in snippets of poetry and song—while the story of hard-working students is lost to history: such, seemingly, is the unchanging nature of student culture over many centuries.

The medieval universities were, in essence, businesses delivering concrete skills and competencies through education to fee-paying students, with individual Masters taking money for lectures given and the university charging for examinations taken (Box 2). They were distinctly utilitarian and vocational, meeting the career aims of their students by opening a door to professional life—there even being an early version of management or business studies, the *dictamen* course. They were certainly not 'ivory towers' devoted to pure scholarship and remote from the needs of providing employable graduates to serve the church, the state, aristocratic landowners, and commerce. The 1379 Foundation Charter for New College, Oxford, duly declares that the university 'has trained many men of great knowledge, beneficial to the Church of God and useful to the King and Kingdom'. While the Masters were very much in charge at Paris as well as at Oxford and Cambridge, the model for the University of Bologna was a guild of students who in effect employed their teachers—even fining them for late-starting or late-finishing lectures (the election of the figure-head rector in the Scottish universities is to this day an echo of such student domination). This was powerful student consumerism: we will note its present-day resurgence later.

Box 2. On the medieval university

The foremost historian researching the universities of the Middle Ages was Hastings Rashdall (a Fellow of New College, Oxford). Here are some examples of the themes he covered in his seminal *The Universities of Europe in the Middle Ages* (1895):

On student life

> The proportion of idle men was perhaps not larger than in most modern universities, but, for the idle, as for the average student in his lighter moods, there was hardly any amusements except drinking, gambling, and singing at taverns; roaming the streets in large gangs under a 'captain' or otherwise, singing, shouting, dancing, throwing stones, breaking doors or heads, and fighting or quarrelling with townsfolk or students of a hostile 'nation'... The violence of medieval university life was almost equalled by its bibulosity.

On student motivation for 'going to uni'

> The brilliant pictures which imaginative historians have sometimes drawn of swarms of enthusiastic students eagerly drinking in the wisdom that fell from the lips of masters have perhaps somewhat blinded us to the fact that the motives which drove men to the university exhibited much the same mixture and much the same variety as they do now... the university was simply the door to the Church; and the door to the Church at that time meant the door to professional life.

On the legacy of the medieval university

> The genius of the Middle Ages showed itself above all in the creation of institutions. The institutions of the Middle Ages are greater—they may prove more imperishable—even than its cathedrals. The university is a distinctly medieval institution.... The very idea of the institution is essentially medieval, and it is curious to observe how largely that idea still dominates our modern schemes of education.

On student control and consumerism at Bologna

Paris and Bologna are the two archetypal—it might be said the only *original* universities: Paris supplied the model for the universities of masters; Bologna for the universities of students...[where the masters] were compelled, under pain of a ban that would have deprived them of pupils and income, to swear obedience to the students' rector, and to obey any other regulations which the universities might think fit to impose upon them...Punctuality is enforced with extreme rigour...[the professor] is forbidden to continue his lecture one minute after the bell has begun to ring for tierce...Even in the actual conduct of his lectures the doctor is regulated with the precision of a soldier on parade or a reader in a French public library.

Beyond Rashdall, a letter from about 1225 written by a student to his father asking for more money appears timeless:

This is to inform you that I am studying at Oxford with great diligence, but the matter of money stands greatly in the way.... The city is expensive...I have to rent lodgings, buy necessaries, and provide for many things which I cannot now specify.

The medieval student is, of course, famously portrayed in Chaucer's *The Canterbury Tales* (1380s) as the five university clerks from Oxford and Cambridge: the almost saintly clerk of Oxford is the idealized version of the studious student who spends all his time and money 'on books and on lernynge', while Nicholas as another clerk is the lusty rascal version of the student. Thus, the Nicholases had to be controlled: the 1292 rules for one Oxford college required that students lead sober lives, 'not fighting, not uttering scurrilous or abusive words, not narrating, singing or eagerly listening to songs or tales about mistresses and loose-living people, or inclining them to lust'; while at New College a century later there were to be 'no pointed shoes and knotted head-gear' worn by its undergraduates.

The rigidity of the medieval method of philosophical and theological enquiry within the universities, known as 'scholasticism', was relaxed as the Renaissance of the 15th and 16th centuries saw the emergence of a modern sense of human identity and of individualism (the *studia humanitatis* based on rhetoric, poetry, history, and moral philosophy). This humanist training in translation, letter-writing, logic, and public speaking amounted to a highly marketable education by way of a sought-after collection of skills and competencies needed within the expanding bureaucracy of church and state. The Enlightenment (or the Age of Reason) of the next two centuries introduced an empirical and experimental approach to learning as the foundation of modern scientific enquiry—but now with developments often happening beyond the universities in places such as Edinburgh's myriad discussion clubs and reading societies; London's Gresham College (1597), with its provision of free public lectures; the Royal Society (1660) and the Royal Institution (1799), with their promotion of science; and the Royal Society of Arts (1754), with its promotion of the application of new learning to commerce and manufacturing as the Industrial Revolution got under way initially in England and then elsewhere across Europe.

In England, Oxford and Cambridge Universities survived the turmoil of Henry VIII and Thomas Cromwell, and then of Oliver Cromwell in the 1640s Civil War. Across Europe, the Master's model (*universitas magistorum*) eclipsed the student-controlled version (*universitas scholarium*), with the output of graduates largely entering the church and later also into the growing state bureaucracies, with sub-sections qualifying in and then practising law or medicine. Thus, the university continued to be firmly linked to the wider society and to the economy in which it found itself, as the nursery of the clergy and of a governing elite.

Not alone, however, Oxford University came in for criticism as it stagnated during the 18th century, its 1750s dons according to Edward Gibbon being 'steeped in port and prejudices'. Adam

Smith in his 1776 famous pioneering study of political economy, *The Wealth of Nations*, lamented the lack of market forces (tuition fees paid direct by the student to the lecturer) in the cosy and cosseted life of the Oxford don who simply receives a set salary from his college, encouraging the performance of teaching duties 'in as careless and slovenly a manner as that authority will permit'—and since the dons were the governing body of the college 'they are likely to make a common cause, to be all very indulgent to one another, and every man to consent that his neighbour may neglect his duty, provided he himself is allowed to neglect his own.' Thus, he went on: 'The discipline of colleges and universities is in general contrived, not for the benefit of the students, but for the interest, or more properly speaking, for the ease of the masters.' Smith would probably have approved of the Bologna *universitas scholarium* and the modern tendency towards student consumerism.

Elsewhere, higher education was showing more dynamism than was apparent in England. Scotland for several hundred years had four universities in Aberdeen, Edinburgh, Glasgow, and St Andrew's to England's Oxford and Cambridge (often jointly referred to as 'Oxbridge' as a term invented by Thackeray in 1849 and only very rarely as 'Camford')—Durham (1832) and the University of London (1836, incorporating University College and King's College created only a few years earlier) being belatedly added to catch up with Scotland; although in fact the London Inns of Court, as other medieval entities, were arguably England's third university, producing common lawyers while Oxford and Cambridge for many centuries focused on canon law and civil law. The Spanish Empire saw the evolving medieval model of the university transplanted from Europe into and across Latin America: Peru, 1551; Mexico, 1551; Bolivia, 1552; Colombia, 1580; Ecuador, 1603; Argentina, 1621—and thence into the Philippines in 1645, Guatemala in 1676, and Cuba in 1721.

The concept of the university as a training institution for the clergy, but also as a finishing-school for young gentlemen, also crossed the Atlantic with the founding of Harvard College as early as 1636—William and Mary College (1693), Yale (1701), Princeton (1747), and Dartmouth (1769) followed. A wider idea of the university as serving the local economy developed with the creation of the first US State universities such as Georgia (1785), North Carolina (1795), and Virginia (1825): they followed more closely the model of the 'useful' Scottish and non-English European universities. The legal difference between US State (i.e. public) universities and private, not-for-profit universities was clarified by the Supreme Court in the 1819 Dartmouth College case, which ensured the survival of the non-public not-for-profit sector that accounts today for some 20 per cent of US higher education (the public universities provide about 75 per cent and the emerging for-profits around 5 per cent). Almost everywhere else, except in the UK where all universities always have been and still are entirely private corporations with the not-for-profit legal status of universities and colleges such as Harvard and Dartmouth, universities tended to become and remain exclusively publicly funded, owned, controlled—often their academics were in effect civil servants employed by the State. The deregulation, liberalization, and quasi-privatization of such institutions has been a theme of change over recent decades across many countries—usually being viewed as politically controversial.

The spread of the university model speeded up from the middle decades of the 19th century—for instance: Sydney (1850) and Melbourne (1853); Calcutta, Madras, and Bombay in 1857; the University of New Zealand (1870); the Imperial Universities of Japan at Tokyo (1877) and Kyoto (1897); Peking (1898), Fudan (1905), and Tsinghua (1911) in China; Cairo (1908), Algiers (1909), and Cape Town (1918) across Africa; and Chulalongkorn (1918) in Thailand. The US also saw a major expansion of universities with the creation of the extensive network of vocational and utilitarian institutions under the far-sighted 1862 Morrill Land-Grant Act, while such progress was rather slower in Europe—and especially in England where the civic universities serving the industrial regions of the Midlands and the North did not emerge until the later 19th century, albeit being built upon local technical colleges dating back to earlier in the century. In the words of the Morrill Act, funds were being provided to establish institutions

> where the leading object shall be, without excluding other scientific and classical studies ... to teach such branches of learning as are related to agriculture and the mechanical arts [hence they are now known as 'A&M' universities] ... in order to promote the liberal and practical education of the industrial classes on the several pursuits and professions in life.

Similarly, in 1900 the promoters of the University of Birmingham declared:

> We desire to systematize and develop the special training required by men in business ... to conduct the great industrial undertakings in the midst of which our work will be done. It is upon the University of Birmingham that falls the responsibility of maintaining the commercial and industrial position of this district.

Such promoters were usually powerful and wealthy local businessmen, notably Joseph Chamberlain in the case of Birmingham.

This utilitarian vision of universities, even if praised by some as being in keeping with their medieval origins, did not escape criticism from the 'ivory tower': Dr Spooner, Warden of New College, fretted that such vocationalism in the form of a 1910s proposal to create Oxford's new-fangled PPE (Politics, Philosophy, Economics) degree might mean that

> too much of the brains and vigour of the country [would end up in the] wealth-amassing career of commerce and business [at the expense of] the more ennobling careers of the clergyman, the student [meaning an academic], the man of science, the teacher, the lawyer, the doctor, and even the public servant.

And Oxford's liberal arts undergraduates came up with the ditty: 'He gets a degree in making jam/At Liverpool and Birmingham'.

If the universities delivered 'higher education' there was also in most countries a strand of 'further education' offered to adults in vocational and technical subjects—notably across the US in the system of community colleges (known as 'junior colleges' until the 1960s) developed during the 20th century and in Europe within technical colleges or polytechnic institutions. We shall explore later whether we should now think more in terms of 'tertiary education' provision for adults, based upon an increasingly wide range of higher and/or further education providers, both traditional public and also recently for-profit organizations. For instance, the university and the polytechnic providers of higher education in the UK were merged in the early 1990s, with the removal of the so-called 'binary line' instantly creating some fifty new universities from the previous polytechnics. Yet, amid such expansion and diversification, the enduring idea of the university remains, perhaps surprisingly, intact—a collection of teachers and students organized into subject areas and functioning in lecture theatres, libraries, and laboratories within often iconic, stylized building structures; safeguarding, disseminating, and creating knowledge; awarding BAs, MAs, and PhDs—as in the Middle Ages.

The ideal of the university has however evolved in a particular way. From a vocational and practical teaching form in its medieval beginnings, intended to supply the church and European States with skilled labour, the early-modern university developed under the influence of the Reformation and Renaissance humanism. The Scientific Revolution and the Enlightenment of the 17th and 18th centuries created new intellectual understandings within universities, which were becoming steadily more secular and now serving the State and commerce more than the church.

Oxford and Cambridge Universities, in the UK, and the US colonial colleges, developed roles of producing educated young gentlemen fit to govern society—as prescribed in Cardinal Newman's 1850s vision of liberal learning for its own sake, set within the college residential model. This influential version of the university—based on Newman's experience of Oxford and its colleges—was set out in his 1852 book, *The Idea of the University*; and is a widely discussed idea of, or ideal for, the university, with its related concept of a liberal education and featuring the Oxford *tutorial* as the favoured means of inculcating critical thinking (in Cambridge, this teaching hour is called *a supervision*).

In contrast, the 19th century, US vocational A&M institutions, supported by Federal legislation, and the UK civic universities, created by local benefactors, were each required to serve industrializing economies by producing graduates with practical skills.

By the middle decades of the 20th century, the university came to be seen by some critics as a more remote 'ivory tower' institution, as taxpayer funding (which began in the UK in 1889 and speeded up with the creation of the Universities Grants Committee in 1919) slowly replaced the need to charge and justify student tuition fees. (Tuition fees have always played a larger role, even in public universities, in the US.)

More recently, in some countries, a reversion to more of a market model for higher education has been seen, as the taxpayer has retreated from financing mass university education and as undergraduate tuition fees have once again become the key source of their income. And along the way there have been critics who have asserted that universities have become too vocational or utilitarian (notably the US state institutions criticized by Abraham Flexner in 1930); and more recently it has been claimed that as part of a 'neo-liberal agenda' they have become too 'marketized', so that higher education has become 'commercialized' and 'commodified'.

Similarly, the ideal of the university as *de facto* (if not strictly *de jure*) controlled by the academics or faculty, by the professors as the academic guild (with each subject area being a veritable sub-guild, or academic tribe, occupying its disciplinary territory) rather than by lay people forming a board of trustees, has changed over the centuries. Ideas about governance have changed: from the autonomous, medieval, academic guild model (where there was nonetheless always the risk of potential interference from the monarch or a bishop); to the formal, theoretical, external control by trustees and overseers in the early US institutions (whose lay founders certainly did not wish to import the English college model of a self-governing academic community); to public control by a government ministry in European universities, especially after the 19th-century spread of centralized Napoleonic state structures and bureaucracies. The earliest text on managing universities—from 1908, by Charles Eliot, the one-time President of Harvard—opens with a chapter on the crucial importance of a balanced relationship between the lay trustees and the faculty as representing the academic guild. Thus, again, we identify Adam Smith's problem of whether to trust self-regulating professionals not to neglect their duties or to seek ways to monitor their activities so as to achieve accountability—or even to impose accountability to the market by way of empowering the student as a fee-paying consumer.

And at the same time the costs of universities increased steadily during the 20th century—partly because they grew more focused on carrying out ever more expensive and increasingly competitive scientific research, a process that meant a change in both the idea of and the ideal form for the university. The idea of the 'research university' is a modern one. The prestige of today's university, or its 'brand value', highlighted in the various global rankings—an industry barely a decade old—depends heavily on the measurement of research outputs rather than on the quality of hard-to-measure teaching. Notably the *OED* definition of 'university' makes no mention of 'research'.

Despite this apparently deepening teaching/research divide, there have been heroic attempts to offer comprehensive, joined-up tertiary education, the most notable being the 1960s California Master Plan, envisaging layers of provision with carefully crafted bridges between them for students to cross the boundaries of the three tiers of the network of well-funded community colleges, the teaching-only campuses of the California State University system, and the research-oriented campuses of the University of California. The Plan was largely the work of Clark Kerr, President of the University of California, who also invented the concept of a 'multiversity' as the modern, large, multi-activity campus in his 1963 book, *The Uses of the University*: these multiversities were institutions 'powered by money' and Kerr accurately predicted—'Which universities get it in the largest quantities will help determine which of them excel in a decade or two' (Box 3). Decades on and in the context of budgetary constraints, the grand ambitions of that Master Plan are seen increasingly as undeliverable. Contemporary with the California Master Plan, in the UK, the 1963 Robbins Report saw the university as: providing 'instruction in skills'; achieving 'the promotion of the general powers of the mind so as to produce not mere specialists but rather cultivated men and women'; seeking 'to maintain research in balance with teaching, since teaching should not be separated from the advancement of learning and the search for truth'; and aiming 'to transmit a common culture and common standards of citizenship'. In the UK, Robbins left the polytechnics, created in the 1960s, to do more of the heavy lifting of delivering vocational courses as 'instruction in skills'.

Now we talk of universities crucially contributing to the 'knowledge society', partly by all delivering a steady flow of graduates as (hopefully) employable human capital; and partly by the creation of economically exploitable intellectual property through the scientific and technological research and innovation that goes on inside them. While the idea and ideal of the medieval university would certainly have recognized the former task of the university,

Box 3. On 'the Idea of a University' as the 1960s multiversity

Clark Kerr (*The Uses of the University*, 1963) is probably next after Newman (Box 4) and alongside Humboldt in setting out an idea and ideal of the modern university—here as the very large, broad-based, multi-activity, post-war, generously government-funded, and research-focused American institution:

> The 'Idea of a University' was a village with its priests. The 'Idea of a Modern University' was a town—a one-industry town—with its intellectual oligarchy. 'The Idea of a Multiversity' is a city of infinite variety...The multiversity has demonstrated how adaptive it [the idea of the university] can be to new opportunities for creativity; how responsive to money; how eagerly it can play a new and useful role; how fast it can change while pretending that nothing has happened at all; how fast it can neglect some of its ancient values.

Kerr was also the architect of the influential and pioneering 1960 California Master Plan for Higher Education, an innovative and progressive scheme creating a comprehensive and high-quality public system carefully linked to the state's network of community colleges so as to maximize accessibility. He became President of the University of California but was dismissed by its Board of Regents amid the student cultural revolution that culminated in the 1968 protests and occupations across the US (notably at Berkeley and Columbia), France (especially at the Sorbonne), Italy (particularly in Milan and Rome), and the UK (notoriously at the London School of Economics (LSE)); see also Box 9.

Alongside the multiversity model, Kerr welcomed an experiment in trying to make the large sprawling institution less impersonal for the undergraduate—the US residential college idea and ideal, very loosely based on the Oxbridge college and seeking to mimic its collegiality and commensality. Attempts had been made at Harvard, Yale, and Princeton, as well as at the California Claremont Colleges, since the 1920s; and in the 1960s the University of California's new Santa Cruz campus carried on the experiment. In essence, however, all such attempts failed to produce anything much more than glorified halls of residence since they came up against the faculty's career stress on research rather than teaching, and also lost out against the organizational dominance of the academic department based on the academic discipline as the best way to organize such research.

In addition, Kerr argued that the development of US higher education drew on two European traditions—the English college with its stress on undergraduate liberal education (Newman and the Oxbridge colleges influencing the early development of Harvard, Yale, and Princeton); and the German, research-focused university with its emphasis on the graduate school (Humboldt and the University of Berlin carried over into the founding of The Johns Hopkins University). But, Kerr adds, the evolution of US higher education involved a third and distinctively American dimension in the creation of the land-grant A&M universities that delivered vocational education and aimed to provide practical solutions to commercial, industrial, and economic problems. Indeed, students over the centuries have usually been more interested in their degree course duly enhancing their employability than in gaining a liberal education within an academically pure idea and ideal of the university. Certainly, the young Americans 'going to college' in the post-war decades as the US achieved the world's first mass publicly funded higher education system were essentially seeking a 'credentializing' process rather than a pure, for-the-sake-of-learning, experience. However much public policy-makers and those within academe may care to view higher education as a social good, the student tends to see it as mainly a private good.

Finally, Kerr famously commented that successfully running a university meant ensuring there was 'sex for the students, parking for the faculty, and football for the alumni'—the last meant a university having teams for semi-professional, competitive sport.

the latter aspect, as we have seen, only began to feature from the later decades of the 19th century. The universities' contribution to science and technology in the two world wars ratcheted up the state funding of the relevant subjects—to a huge extent in the US. In the context of mass higher education in Western countries from the second half of the 20th century, the challenge for today's policy-makers and for individual universities is how to balance the demands of pursuing the kudos of research while trying not to neglect the once prime teaching mission. How may universities earn prestige via the global rankings measuring research while also being sure of 'selling' their undergraduate student places (at increasingly high prices by way of tuition fees) where 'student satisfaction' scores and teaching rankings influence applicants' selection of their university?

Elsewhere in the world beyond the US and the UK, the process of steady expansion of universities during the early decades of the 20th century and then especially from the 1960s has been the norm for Canada, Australia, and most European countries. A transition to mass higher education has also been usual at some point for almost all systems in the second half of the last century, involving the creation of new public institutions and in some countries the entrance of private providers (whether charitable not-for-profit or commercial for-profit) as a way of absorbing demand where public funding was not available to expand the traditional sector. This has been particularly noticeable in the US, China, Latin America, and Eastern Europe. And in recent decades, limitations on local provision have been overcome through a developing global student market, drawing students notably from China, India, and other Asian countries to pay high tuition fees for degree courses in the US, UK, and Australian universities: the roaming scholar of 12th-century Europe is back, travelling by air.

Other countries seek to enter the international students market, offering to teach in English; while US and UK universities expand this market by opening branch campuses in Asia and in the

Middle East, often with a local partner. Another area of growth has been in the provision of taught Master's degrees, where often the political limits to the fees that can be charged to local undergraduates do not apply—the many and sometimes very expensive MBA courses are a prime example. The modern university, whether public or private, now acts far more like a business than it did even in the recent past, needing faster moving and more skilled managers. Such a change in the internal culture gives rise to fears among the professors or faculty of losing their hard-won power within the organizational hierarchy, especially as universities use more and more part-time, temporary teachers ('adjuncts') to replace full-time academics.

The rest of this book goes on to explore: just what the modern university does by way of teaching, research, consultancy, and wider civic engagement activity; the various patterns of higher education around the world; how the university actually works in terms of its structures and funding, governance and management; where its students fit in—who is selected, how they get through, and what happens when they get out as graduates; and what working in universities is like. The future, addressed in our final chapter, will probably entail a continuing and enduring idea of the university, but, as in the past, in a changing ideal form. That might include disruptive change arising from, say, the continued reduction of public funding per student—or perhaps from as yet unknown innovations turning out to be the long-awaited productivity game-changer that will transform higher education. Or will there be change by way of steady reform—albeit never perhaps enough change to satisfy higher education's critics?

Chapter 2
What do universities and colleges do?

Teaching and research—the key functions

While the work of universities is of consuming interest to those who spend much of their lives in them, it is largely a mystery to those outside them. This is at least partly because the simple question in the chapter title, fairly easy to answer for most types of organizations and institutions, becomes, for universities, more complicated the more it is probed.

For most universities, everywhere in the world, their main task is teaching high-school leavers (and some other young and not-so-young people) to first-degree level (the awards have different names in different countries), typically requiring three or four years of full-time study or an equivalent part-time period. Across Europe, governments are trying to standardize this period—a matter of particular concern in countries where the duration has crept up to five, six, or even seven years. (This standardization is known as the *Bologna Process*.) One of the seeming paradoxes of university life is that this central task of first-degree teaching, on which everything else in higher education depends, is usually regarded as the least prestigious academic work, often given to the most junior academic staff or even to students studying for higher degrees; and universities that do little else are, in most places, considered to be lower status institutions. It has, of course, been widely recognized that this is an undesirable state of affairs on many levels, but efforts to change it have usually met with only limited success—because of the power of the various status hierarchies which we will describe here.

The other two best-known, and connected, functions of universities are research and postgraduate teaching—a third, called 'service' in the US, exists in terms of academe and academics contributing to the economy and community. These are the higher status academic tasks, and in most countries tend to be concentrated in higher status universities; although (in most national higher education systems) nearly all universities do at least some work in both these fields. The dynamics relating to research, and postgraduate teaching to some extent, help to explain the paradox about first-degree teaching. People usually enter academic life because of an intellectual passion for a subject. This means that they want to pursue some aspects of the subject to their known limits (which is what postgraduate study is intended to do) and then advance beyond them (through research). While first-degree teaching poses both intellectual challenges (understanding the essence of the subject) and pedagogic ones (presenting this understanding in a clear and engaging way), they are of a different nature to receiving international recognition for an original contribution to one's subject, probably with career advancement and perhaps also with personal financial gain, and possibly with important implications beyond academic life. It is easy to see why research becomes a high-prestige activity around which much university life revolves.

In the last few decades, the growth of higher education around the world, its increased costs, and the greater international mobility of students have led to more interest in classifying universities—creating rankings, or 'league tables'. There are positive aspects to this (students have something to go on other than universities' self-promotions when making choices, and institutional managements may be held to account for a lowly ranking) and negative aspects (they may, as with leagues in sports, tend to solidify institutional hierarchies, and measure only the easily measurable, and may also be based on a particular idea of an 'ideal' university). Because research intensity is often thought of as a proxy for quality more generally, and also because research is readily quantifiable in terms of inputs (research budgets) or outputs (the extent to which research work is referred to by other scholars as 'citations' in journals or books, or generates income through patents and the licensing of intellectual property discovered or invented inside the university), or in other ways, it tends to play a large part in determining universities' positions in rankings. Thus, the desire of individual academics to contribute to their subject becomes interwoven with institutional imperatives to generate additional income through research and at the same time to improve ranking positions, leading to research being accorded its high-status position. Being seen as a 'research university' has relatively recently become a top accolade—as we will see later in this book.

We must emphasize here that there is a widely held view that universities can be 'good' in various ways: they do many things, and obsessing about one of their functions—research—is, we suggest, unhelpful to understanding their place in complex, modern societies. While academic work, including research, has always had a competitive edge, it is usually balanced by a practical need for collaboration (especially in the sciences). Moreover, the seductive comparison between sports leagues and university rankings is invalid. Nobody—other than ardent supporters—disputes that the best football teams are those that score most goals. But no such indisputable and simple single measure is available with which to judge universities—or, for that matter, many other institutions serving society, such as hospitals and schools.

Research work is sometimes contrasted with scholarship, although the two usually complement one another. For academic staff, scholarship involves keeping abreast of the latest thinking in their subject through reading, attending conferences, and involvement in seminars. In some humanities subjects, where data collection through laboratory or fieldwork does not take place, scholarship and research may merge into one another. It is an open, and hotly contested, question whether high-quality teaching requires teachers to be active in research, but up-to-date scholarship is certainly essential for good teaching.

Postgraduate teaching occupies an intermediate position between first-degree teaching and research. In most countries, postgraduate teaching is mainly for Master's degrees, which may consist largely of taught courses with some original research by way of submitting a dissertation; or may be more research-oriented by way of submitting a thesis. Master's courses are generally of one or two years' full-time study (or equivalent part-time periods) and usually require a relevant first degree to provide the intellectual foundations for higher level work. A small number of students with Master's degrees then go on to take Doctoral degrees. This is usually a Doctor of Philosophy degree—regardless of the subject being studied—commonly abbreviated to PhD (sometimes DPhil). In recent years, what are known as professional Doctorates have developed in areas such as engineering, law, education, and business studies. Doctoral degrees usually require at least three years' full-time study or five to seven years' part-time work. The student identifies a specific research topic—agreed in consultation with the member of academic staff who will guide the student, and who is known either as a supervisor or an advisor—and produces a thesis of typically between 50,000 and 100,000 words on the results of their study. Sometimes, the student will be a junior member of a research team, and their thesis will form a contribution to the larger research project. The thesis is intended to demonstrate the student's technical abilities as a researcher, as well as a high level of intellectual ability (and professional expertise if it is a professional Doctorate). It, therefore, has a particular, formal character, to a greater extent than even a specialist academic book would typically have. Obtaining a

Doctoral degree is, in most countries, a prerequisite to obtaining an academic post—although most Doctoral students go on to professional or other careers outside universities.

In the European university tradition there are 'Higher Doctorates' (Doctor of Science (DSc), for example) awarded to senior academics during the course of their careers to signify an unusually important and sustained intellectual contribution to their specialist field. In some continental European countries, 'Habilitated' Doctorates (often abbreviated to 'Dr Hab') may, rather similarly, be awarded, and are often a requirement for academic advancement.

One difficulty that we have had in writing this book—already noted—has been to make appropriate references to countries whose higher education systems have different characteristics to those with which the authors are most familiar. However, it is surely remarkable that the Bachelor-Master-Doctor classification of academic achievement—which is, of course, an entirely arbitrary one—is truly global (and, in essence, dates from the earliest universities founded in the Middle Ages). Universities around the world are all similar, yet all different.

Slicing the university cake

This account of what universities do slices the academic cake vertically, so to speak, with different slices for first-degree teaching, research, and so on. But we may also think of universities' work in terms of horizontal slices through the cake.

One horizontal slice, running through first-degree and postgraduate teaching, scholarship, and some types of research, would reveal what is sometimes called the *emancipatory model* of higher education, or the idea of liberal higher education. Many academics and others would consider this to be the essential feature of universities, distinguishing them from institutions of vocational education or specialist research institutes: it is what makes them special. This is the task of helping students to form their own understandings of the world, reflecting on the ideas of important thinkers in the humanities and sciences from different eras and different cultures. The notions of critical thinking—*criticality*—and autonomy are crucial here. Emancipatory higher education expects students not merely to understand the ideas of earlier, and perhaps current, thinkers but to engage with them critically, to challenge their ideas—which does not necessarily imply disagreement—so as to embody the ideas in question, no doubt in changed form, in their own views of the world. They then, ideally, become intellectually autonomous, drawing on a deep knowledge of other thinkers, incorporated into their own perspectives: they learn how to learn, how to refresh their ideas, and how to address new challenges throughout their lives (Box 4).

Box 4. On 'the idea of a university' as 1850s Oxford

John Henry, Cardinal Newman (1801–90) set out probably the most famous concept of the idea and ideal of the university, especially in relation to the value of a 'Liberal Education' (as against a vocational education):

A habit of mind is formed which lasts through life, of which the attributes are, freedom, equitableness, calmness, moderation, and wisdom... [all] as the special fruit of the education found at a University... [this] Liberal Education, viewed in itself, is simply the cultivation of the intellect, as such, and its object is nothing more or less than intellectual excellence... This process of training, by which the intellect, instead of being formed or sacrificed to some particular or accidental purpose, some specific trade or profession, or study or science, is disciplined for its own sake, for the perception of its own proper object, and for its own highest culture, is called Liberal Education... And to set forth the right

(continued)

Box 4. Continued

standard, and to train according to it, and to help forward all students towards it according to their various capacities, this I conceive to be the business of a University . . . a University training is the great ordinary means to a great but ordinary end; it aims at raising the intellectual tone of society, at cultivating the public mind, at supplying true principles to popular enthusiasm and fixed aims to popular aspirations, at giving enlargement and sobriety to the ideas of the age.

Newman wanted the university to prepare 'Gentlemen as Leaders'—see also Box 8. 'Liberal Education', he declared, makes 'the gentleman' and:

It is well to be a gentlemen, it is well to have a cultivated intellect, a delicate taste, a candid, equitable, dispassionate mind, a noble and courteous bearing on the conduct of life—these are the connatural qualities of a large knowledge; they are the objects of a University.

Comparable to Newman in terms of leaving an influential legacy for thinking about the university are Kerr (Box 3) on the 'Multiversity' and also Humboldt on the concept of *Bildung*—the university as a holistic, democratic, questioning community of scholars (professors and students) pursuing life-long intellectual self-cultivation and self-development; both Newman and Humboldt would see a university education as being far more than merely a matter of gaining a credential to enhance vocational employability.

Another horizontal slice would reveal the *professional formation model* for a university. This has been a central task of universities since they emerged in Europe in the 11th and 12th centuries, and remains so today, in all countries. Most university students are bound for a profession, in the broad sense of the term, even those not studying an obviously professional course such as medicine, law, or engineering. Few history students become professional historians, but many do enter careers where the analytical and presentational skills of the historian are in demand. Universities in Britain and elsewhere have helped to create 'modern' professions such as town planning or social work by developing degree courses in these fields which have helped to define professional boundaries and standards, and the acquisition of these degrees has often become a prerequisite for professional practice. Meanwhile, older professions such as accountancy, architecture, teaching, and nursing have moved from an apprenticeship model of professional development to one where a university qualification embodying both theoretical knowledge and relevant skills in the subject is a frequent starting point.

The professional formation slice through the university takes in first-degree and postgraduate teaching, and related research and consultancy activities. The distinctive US model in this area requires a first degree with relevant specializations before moving on to graduate school (in the same, or a different, university) where professional formation in medicine, law, business, or other fields, takes place at postgraduate level. This model clearly increases the costs (actual, as fees, and in terms of income forgone) to the individual in search of professional qualification, but is being experimented with in countries such as Australia (and, very tentatively, in the UK). Although at first sight very different from the traditional British route to professional qualification, there are hidden similarities. The university degree in Britain does not in itself usually provide a 'licence to practice' as it does, after longer degree courses, in some other European countries. Instead, cost-sharing models with the relevant professions have grown up, under which completion of a degree course which meets the requirements of the professional body concerned is the route to a junior role practising the profession under supervision from senior professionals (in a hospital or in an engineering firm, for example), leading to recognition by the professional body after perhaps two or three years. The 'graduate school' is thus instead provided by the profession itself.

One recent trend has been for corporate 'universities' to be established—in effect, usually corporate training centres with grandiose titles. The 'McDonald's Hamburger University', located near Chicago, is one of the best-known examples: according to its website, 'Training at Hamburger University has emphasized consistent restaurant operations procedures, service, quality and cleanliness. It has become the company's global centre of excellence for McDonald's operations training and leadership development.' While these goals are clearly worthwhile ones from the company's point of view, they fall some way short of what has been traditionally expected from an institution with the university title and one properly engaged in what makes higher education higher. Other large corporations have at various times had the idea of developing more academically-focused institutions than in the McDonald's case, but seem to have generally concluded that the costs would outweigh the possible benefits—especially once it is realized that existing universities are glad to devise courses tailor-made for their industry's training and development needs.

Another horizontal slice through the higher education cake shows the university as society's principal research engine. This takes in research activity itself, of course, but also postgraduate work that may be integrated with research projects. In some countries—Germany is the example usually given of this working well—much research takes place outside universities in specialist research institutions (such as Germany's Max Planck Institutes). The former Soviet Union carried out most of its research in specialist institutes grouped under the Academy of Sciences, and this model is continued in many of the countries that came at various times within the old Soviet sphere of influence, including China. In many other countries, there are specialist research institutes placed within universities and with varying degrees of integration with the mainstream university activities, but much research is also carried on within departments that teach first-degree and postgraduate students. There are believed to be a number of advantages in locating research under the control of more general-purpose universities. For one thing, costly resources such as laboratories, scientific equipment, and libraries may be used more intensively if they can serve a larger group of users. For another, academic staff often remark on how their research has helped to inform their teaching; and, sometimes, that having to revisit basic concepts through teaching has sparked new thoughts that may lead to research ideas. People who were once effective researchers may become less productive as the years go by, and being able to move easily into a primarily teaching role allows their accumulated knowledge to be exploited in a different way. Drawing too sharp a distinction between teaching and research is, in any case, for many academics, practically unhelpful and intellectually incoherent: both are about the use and extension of knowledge (Humboldt's *Bildung*).

The disciplinary idea

Students generally come to university to study one or more subjects (indeed sampling many subjects in the US before fixing on their 'major' and 'minor' academic interests); and these subjects—academics like to call them 'disciplines'—form the basis of university organization. Even in the more broadly based US liberal arts college model, described in Chapter 3, students usually major in one subject. We noted in Chapter 1 the core curriculum common to medieval universities in Europe; the modern university that emerged in 19th-century Europe and the US was based around a new idea of what the disciplinary basis of universities should be, including the natural sciences, the developing social sciences, and modern languages. Medicine, previously taught in hospitals on an apprenticeship model, was brought into universities as the development of scientific medicine showed the need to link what happened in laboratories to what happened on the hospital ward. What are, and what are not, 'university subjects' remains a matter of debate, linked to changing ideas about the nature of knowledge itself. The inclusion of engineering, for instance, in British university curricula in the later decades of the 19th century was considered revolutionary at the time; late 20th-century parallels could be media studies or sports science.

Academics mostly consider themselves to have a disciplinary affiliation. This 'home discipline' usually provides the set of understandings and concepts that informs their intellectual engagement with the world of ideas more broadly, even if they may not be involved actively in teaching or researching mainly in that discipline. Physics, history, and economics are examples of disciplines. These are divided into sub-disciplines—theoretical physics, medieval history, macroeconomics—and academics (again, typically) spend their working lives in one of this growing number of sub-disciplines. As knowledge progresses, new areas for study appear, often requiring contributions from more than one discipline, and which over time may come to be seen as disciplines in their own right, with their own intellectual regularities: biochemistry or economic history. Equally, disciplines once seen as fundamental may lose their leading roles as the structure of knowledge changes and they may be subsumed within other areas of study—botany is an example. Other areas of knowledge which require inputs from different disciplines may not develop into separate disciplines, but may continue to be seen as *interdisciplinary* (or *transdisciplinary*—there is a technical distinction) fields. Area studies, where knowledge from economics, sociology, political science, and other fields is focused to help understand particular regions (South-East Asia or Latin America, say), is an example of interdisciplinary study, as is, say, urban studies.

University managements have the task of making organizational sense of what are inevitably untidy, and changing, groupings of knowledge. A common approach is to create a set of discipline-based *departments*, and then to group these into what may be called *faculties* or *schools* (e.g. the School of Humanities; the Faculty of Science and Engineering). (A regular source of confusion is the US use of the term 'faculty' to mean the academic staff of a university and the European use to mean an organizational unit.) In large universities, a three-tier structure often exists, with faculties being grouped into a small number of schools (or the terms may be reversed). In some universities, the department is the more significant organizational entity, with important decisions about teaching, research, staff, students, and money being made there; in other places, the faculty or the school is the more significant location or organizational unit.

Because there is no single correct solution to the problem of how to organize knowledge-based organizations, university structures are the subject of almost constant review and change (Box 5)—although most ordinary members of academic staff continue with their teaching and research, in their subject-based work group, often relatively unaffected by changes going on around them in the organization. The academic 'department' usually remains a fairly stable feature of a university's structure—its basic building block.

Box 5. On the emerging discontent with the 1960s expansion of higher education

Andrew Davies, in his UK campus novel (*A Very Peculiar Practice*, 1986) about a new doctor (Stephen) joining the university's medical practice and here being inducted by a jaded colleague (Bob), neatly captures the growing disenchantment with the recent expansion of higher education and the creation of the 'new universities' on greenfield campuses such as Warwick, Essex, Kent, York, and Lancaster:

'Let me tell you about this terrible place, Stephen. They call it a new university, but it's twenty years old now. Novelty value's worn off, it's way down the pecking order. Concrete's crumbling, all those bloody silly flat roofs leak, tiles falling off walls on to people's heads, we've got a repair budget

(continued)

Box 5. Continued

four times the total salary bill...I'll tell you what it's like. It's like a very, very inefficient sector of British industry. The plant's an obsolete slum, top management's totally corrupt and idle, middle management's incompetent and idle, and the workforce are bolshy and idle. And, of course, there's no bloody product. No wonder people get ill here. There's nothing else for them to do.'...Lowlands University, it appeared, was a shithole.

Bradbury (1975, *The History Man*—see Box 9) describes the 'new' 1960s University of Watermouth: 'In the rain the buildings are bleak; the concrete has stained; the glass grown dirty; the services diminished. The graffiti experts have been at work...'.

Chapter 3
Global patterns of higher education

Types of higher education systems

Around the world, universities vary greatly, but also have much in common. This paradox forms the basis of much of the scholarship and research about higher education, allowing comparative study of institutions which differ but have similar basic forms. The various international ratings of universities (discussed further in Chapter 4) draw whatever plausibility they have from a widely held assumption that universities in America and in, say, China, share enough important features to allow measurement on a common scale.

Although virtually every country in the world has its own national higher education system, and each of these national systems has its own peculiarities (and most national systems contain considerable variations within them), scholars of higher education have managed to fit them all into a small number of system types. This small number of types results from several factors: the rippling-out of early ideas about the university through, and then beyond, Western Europe; the imposition of standard university organizational forms by colonial powers (European states from the 17th to the early 20th centuries; and the Soviet Union during the 20th century), with the universities long outliving the colonial structures that created them, but usually adhering broadly to their original colonial model; and the emulation by developing countries of what they see as successful models elsewhere (often looking to the US). What we view today in higher education, around the world, is the result of the vagaries of global history; but these system types are all based on a broad common understanding of what higher education is—or at least, should be.

Despite the idea of the university emerging in 11th- and 12th-century Europe, the universities that we see today are all modern in the sense that they are based upon essentially 19th-century ideas about teaching, research, and scholarship. In most universities now, only the academic robes and the mace (and sometimes the buildings) suggest a link to the Middle Ages. The few exceptions to this rule include the University of al-Qarawiyyin in Morocco (mentioned in Chapter 1) and the Al-Azhar University in Cairo, founded in the 10th century, and both still operating today as centres of Islamic scholarship. Other ancient higher education systems—the Chinese one, for example, can be traced back over several thousand years—were re-created in relatively recent times (the Chinese system in 1895) to conform with newer ideas about what a university should be. European universities with medieval origins—Paris and Oxford, for example—re-invented themselves, or had re-invention imposed on them, variously in the 19th and 20th centuries, as society changed and new forms of knowledge appeared, to become the important modern institutions that we now see.

What led to this global common understanding of what a university should be?

The economic and political changes that swept Europe in the early 19th century led to the creation of a new type of university in Germany, with its model being the University of Berlin, founded in 1811 and directed initially by the philosopher and educationist Wilhelm von Humboldt. This type of university, which became known as the Humboldtian model, emphasized the integration of teaching and research, and the freedom of its professors to organize the two as they saw fit, and also their students' academic freedom (the concepts of *Lehrfreiheit* and *Lernfreiheit*). This gave rise to the 'chair' system, influential still today in the national systems which adopted the Humboldtian model, under which senior professors gathered a group of junior staff around them, rather than organizing through academic departments: these exist, but they are less central than in other organizational models. Although these new German universities were state institutions (and they remain so today), it was understood that the role of the state was to safeguard academic freedom rather than to impose political constraints: academic self-government thus became a key feature of the Humboldtian model, and continues to be seen by many commentators as a defining characteristic of a 'real' university.

German universities became important centres for scientific research in the 19th and early 20th century, particularly in chemistry and physics (with close links to industry), and developed the PhD degree as the standard for high-level research training. This model became highly influential across Europe and in the US. The professors of the University of London, created in 1836, looked to Germany for progressive models of university organization—rather than to the two long-established English universities, Oxford and Cambridge. The Johns Hopkins University, founded in Baltimore, Maryland, in 1876, is generally considered to be the first American university to adopt the Humboldtian model of advanced scholarship and PhD programmes—although its example was not widely copied by other US universities until the 20th century.

Germany's was not the only continental European model for higher education, however. France provided the so-called 'Napoleonic' model: state-controlled as in the German model, but without its emphasis on academic self-government. The purpose of the university was to serve the state by providing skilled graduates, rather than to allow professors to pursue their own academic objectives. (The two may not necessarily be mutually exclusive, of course.) The pinnacles of the French model were (and remain) the *grandes écoles*. The *École Normale Supérieure* and the *École Polytechnique* were creations of the French Revolution, established in the 1790s, but the tradition dates back to earlier in the 18th century when the *École d'Arts et Métiers* and the *École des Ponts et Chaussées*, among others, were established. Below this top tier, universities were directed centrally rather as if they were government departments, with little scope for variation in the curriculum and with academic staff appointments being handled centrally. This model was exported to the countries that came under French control or influence in the Napoleonic wars at the start of the 19th century (notably Spain, Portugal, and Italy), and later also to France's African colonies.

What is usually referred to as the British higher education system consisted until the early 19th century of just two English universities—Oxford and Cambridge—and four Scottish ones: in order of establishment, St Andrews, Glasgow, Aberdeen, and Edinburgh. Then came the Universities of Durham (1832) and London (1836), the latter incorporating the recently founded institution that became University College London, and King's College London. Most other European states had more extensive higher education systems by this time, usually including institutions specializing in engineering and other technologies—something absent in Britain until the 20th century—as well as 'classical' universities dealing with pure science and the humanities. English higher education began to expand in the booming cities of the Industrial Revolution—which had taken place without any input from universities, although aided by such philosophical and scientific societies as the Lunar Society in Birmingham. These so-called 'civic' universities were created by local initiatives in Manchester (Figure 3), Liverpool, Leeds, Birmingham, Bristol, and elsewhere, usually starting their lives

3. The University of Manchester main building (1873; by Alfred Waterhouse)—the typical clock-tower and civic-pride architecture of the Victorian and Edwardian expansion of universities (often still combined with the older iconic quadrangle; see Figure 1).

as colleges (Owens College, founded in 1851, in the case of Manchester, for example) without degree-awarding powers.

These newer universities differed from Oxford and Cambridge by having both more modern curricula and governing bodies which were distinct from their academic communities, and which oversaw the general direction of each institution. They were private rather than state organizations, small (the whole of the University of London, the largest British university

4. Senate House, University of London (1938; by Charles Holden)—the building makes a statement as the headquarters of an imperial university.

of the time, had fewer than 2,000 students by 1900; most universities would have had a few hundred students) but with strong local roots. Funding depended on local goodwill and income from student fees: central government funding—as distinct from local municipal support—for higher education in Britain expanded in a systematic way only in the 1920s, and initially at very modest levels. This organizational approach—creating what would now be called third-sector bodies, private but with public accountability, and the separation of general governance (particularly financial control) from academic decision-making—became known as the Anglo-Saxon model. The distinctiveness of these universities was typically signalled by the granting of a Royal Charter, which established the university as a corporate entity with the usual powers of a business corporation, and with, crucially, degree-awarding powers. The Anglo-Saxon legacy can still be seen around the world in the organization of universities in former British imperial possessions, including Canada, Australia, New Zealand, and many African and Asian countries. Currently the leading universities of Singapore and of Hong Kong, founded on this model, are outperforming most other Asian universities.

The pattern of higher education in the US has always been diverse: there has never been a national system as such. The Oxford and Cambridge model was exported to Britain's North American colonies, and formed the basis for one type of university organization. Private higher education developed in the pre-and post-revolutionary eras, with large-scale (for the period) university development following from the Morrill Act of 1862 (passed by Congress at the height of the Civil War, it should be noted), which established the so-called 'land grant' universities, funded by the sale of federal lands in the expanding US. These were, and remain, institutions directly controlled by the states, with original missions to support the economic development of the states in which they were located. Many have developed into leading universities such as the state universities of California, Michigan, and Wisconsin. This US model influenced undergraduate developments in early 20th-century China.

There are a number of variations to this general picture: the Scandinavian countries developed a university model which emphasizes egalitarian values, while the former Soviet Union's model created industry-related universities (petroleum engineering, railways, agronomy, and so on) which were often placed under the control of the ministry responsible for that industry, rather than the ministry of education. The armed forces also usually had their own university-level institutions. And some consider there to be an emerging Confucian model in certain Asian countries, to be set alongside the Humboldtian model of Germany and the Nordic states; the Napoleonic model found in France, Spain, Italy, and much of Latin America; the US's Ivy League and intensive research model, along with its public flagship state university campuses; and the English form of the university spread across the former British Empire.

These different patterns of higher education, interacting with one another through the international movement of academic staff and students, and through 'policy borrowing' by governments seeking to emulate apparently more successful higher education projects elsewhere, have moved during the later 20th century to produce, arguably, a standard university model (at least, a widely adopted one): one of strong multi-faculty universities with a significant degree of autonomy from central government. These are the universities—the thirty to fifty or so *world class universities* (WCUs) or *super research universities* (SRUs) that are at the top of most university rankings tables (with a few exceptions in the form of small, high-quality specialist institutions), and is the model promoted by international agencies as being supposedly the most effective for academic achievement and also for supporting economic development.

Institutional types

Because most universities do most—often, all—of the tasks noted in Chapter 2, they cannot be placed in neat categories: what are often referred to as 'research universities', for example, usually get most of their income from teaching. The expansion of higher education around the world in the last half-century has made classification even harder, with every country having a distinctive pattern, even though they can be made to fit (with a bit of pushing) into the four or five general groupings that we have described.

Research universities, so-called, are generally considered to form an elite group in most national higher education systems. Usually, one or two universities can be thought of (certainly, they think this themselves) as 'apex' institutions (so-called WCUs), the ones that set the standards for the rest of the national system (in some cases, globally) and which the most able students, researchers, and academic staff aspire to join. It is easy to see how such institutions can sustain their reputations, if they are able to suck in the cream of national—and to an increasing extent international—student and academic talent, as well as to attract large amounts of research funding as a consequence. Who would go to a lesser regarded university as a student or as a staff member if they were able to go to a top-ranked one? (The more difficult trick to pull off is to gain this 'apex' position in the first place: there is a brisk international trade in advice on this.) Some refer to these universities at the apex of various nations' pyramids of prestige as the elite *emerging global model* universities (the EGMs), having more in common with each other in being research-centred, prestige-seeking entities than with the universities below them within their own national hierarchy of institutions, and especially with those that are the teaching-only, reputation-seeking institutions at the base of the pyramid. Awkwardly squeezed between the small apex and the broad base is a middle layer of aspiring universities, hoping one day to join the elites that are, say, America's Ivy League, the UK's Russell Group, Australia's Sandstones. In some countries, where the system is not highly stratified or segmented, the pyramid is fairly flat, without so many distinct levels (typically in the Nordic countries).

The elite 'top' universities are thus able to be highly selective in their student intakes, which in most countries favours young people from upper or middle class backgrounds, whose parents were able to give them a good start in life. (At various times in the former Soviet Union and China, ideological imperatives led to preferential access to higher education for the children of 'workers': the same principle applied, however—the apex universities were recruiting from a favoured section of the population, as determined by the ruling political party.) Academic and social status thus become intertwined, with the graduates of apex universities typically gaining leading positions in national and international business, politics, government, the media, and so on—and thereby supposedly justifying the correctness of the universities' admissions policies. These elite universities can be seen as a mechanism for perpetuating a socio-economic elite class with, in some places, an added dimension of ethnic or gender preference, thus giving rise to lively political debates about widening access to them in order to address social inequalities.

Today we can also identify a set of SRUs within which there is arguably a top-most echelon, positioned ahead even of the other 'super' universities, with large endowments (that is, capital funds built up over the years, available to the university to spend as it wishes): Harvard (with an endowment of over $35 billion), Stanford, Princeton, Yale, MIT, Oxford, Cambridge, and Berkeley. These universities are to be found in 'creative clusters', in cities that 'buzz': Boston, with Harvard and MIT; San Francisco, with Stanford and Berkeley; and 'the golden triangle' of London (with University College London and Imperial College as its global leaders), Oxford, and Cambridge. It is worth mentioning that

Stanford, founded only in the 1890s, has surged to the fore as a global top-ten institution mainly on the back of the US government's funding of scientific research during the Second World War and later (it has been called 'the Cold War University'), and more recently on huge donations to its hefty endowment. Stanford annually receives about $500 million of Federal government research funds, as do the University of Michigan, the University of Wisconsin-Madison, and the University of California at Berkeley. But SRUs in China and other Asian countries are climbing the league tables, especially as in some countries government funding of higher education is deliberately aimed at creating world-class universities (possibly at the expense of the rest of the national higher education system). In all such research-focused universities (some 200 in the US and about twenty-five in the UK), and also in some US small liberal arts colleges, as in the Oxbridge colleges, the faculty guild manages the search for and the working conditions of academics—there is a collegial or shared-values style of governance, even if so-called 'donnish dominion' is not as strong as it was in the 1960s.

A distinctively American model has been the liberal arts college or university: usually private, often high-status, focusing on a reputation for high-quality undergraduate teaching rather than on research as the exclusive currency of prestige. Students often go on to prestigious graduate schools or to postgraduate work in research universities. The model has appealed to other countries seeking an alternative to the research (high-status) / teaching (low-status) dichotomy, but with apparently very limited success: an example of how a seemingly attractive educational arrangement in one country can be difficult to transplant to a different educational, social, and economic climate. Similarly, the 'Honors Program' (extra teaching for a carefully selected 10–15 per cent of undergraduates) found in some large US public universities seems, so far, not to have spread much beyond the US (other than, to some extent, into a few universities in the Netherlands).

A development over the last half-century in Western Europe, and found in different forms in Africa, Asia, and Latin America, has been the emergence of the regional university. These are institutions created by the state to support economic development in underprivileged regions, sometimes with the aim of slowing population loss by providing education locally and attracting new enterprises by drawing on the university's resources. This is in fact a long-established model of university development, with the American 'land grant' universities, created by the Morrill Act of 1862 with the intention of helping to develop the new states of the American West, being a prime example. In England, what are now often called the 'civic universities' were established by local initiatives in the industrial cities of Victorian England to provide skilled manpower for local businesses, but also with an idea of uplifting the city's cultural standards. Similar examples can be taken from across industrializing 19th-century Europe.

The usual idea of a university is of an institution that includes many subjects, arts and sciences, in its curriculum. But there is also a long tradition of specialized, or *monotechnic*, institutions, pursuing just one area of work. Medicine and law are cases where medieval schools in these fields were established in Europe and in some cases continued as separate institutions into the modern period. Some of the London medical schools, for instance, long pre-dated the University of London of which they eventually became part. In the 19th century, in Europe and America, colleges specializing in art and design, engineering, agriculture, education, and other professional fields, as well as performance-based institutions in music and drama, were established. In some countries, this tradition of specialist institutions has continued to the present day, whereas in others (the UK is a leading example) most have merged with a university (in some cases retaining a degree of independent existence but in many cases not). In medicine, mergers were driven by advances in medical science and the consequent impossibility of relatively small institutions being able adequately to teach the range of scientific developments which underlie current medical practice. In other fields, the advantages of being part of a large institution in an increasingly complex and competitive higher education environment seemed to outweigh the benefits of independence.

Universities are associated in most people's minds with a distinctive physical manifestation. Not for nothing are the leading American east coast universities known as the Ivy League—the association of gothic architecture (the real thing or a later imitation) with higher education has been a source of fascination to scholars of both architecture and higher education for some time. But not all students are part of a university like this; some rarely (perhaps never) actually even set foot in theirs. These are the so-called 'distance-learning' students, being taught and learning in a way that is now largely based on computers and the Internet but which goes back to 19th-century postal-based systems. The University of London's 'external system' provided opportunities for students around the world to gain a London degree from the 1850s: most of them were taught in colleges in Asian and African countries of the then British Empire, which usually went on to become leading universities in their post-colonial nations.

The UK's Open University (the OU), founded in 1969, was a pioneer in developing distance learning, initially sending teaching materials by post supplemented by in-person tutorial support and later using television as its main teaching medium to supplement its course packs. It provided a route into higher education for people who for a variety of reasons were unable to attend in person what were then a much smaller number of universities. The OU may be seen as a 1960s development of a long tradition aimed at meeting the needs of people unable to experience the luxury of what the scholar Michael Oakeshott called the 'gift of an interval' (though, of course, full-time students never seem to see it that way). This tradition goes back to 19th-century initiatives which included 'philosophical and literary societies', 'working men's institutes' (several of which provided the historical foundations for the civic universities of the 1900s and later for the 1960s polytechnics), and Birkbeck College in London, which has provided evening higher education teaching since 1823.

More recent distance-learning developments include the provision of MOOCs—*massive open-access online courses*—based on the idea that most of the teaching materials now used by universities are digitally based, and could, therefore, be made available online at minimal cost to the university and the user. Although initially seen by some commentators as a 'game-changer' for higher education (after all, who would study at an obscure university when they could apparently obtain a qualification for next-to-nothing from a famous university such as Stanford or MIT?), their impact has, so far, been rather slight (as 'edutainment'). Higher education study turns out to be a social activity within the context of a specific institution as much as anything else. Even so, if major employers were ever to accept a package of MOOCs which had received some form of accreditation as being a degree-equivalent credential, then MOOCs might generate the disruptive innovation that some commentators have predicted.

Public and private

Universities may be classed as either public or private, and in many places the difference is highly significant: the US is the prime example, with many—but by no means all—of its elite institutions such as Harvard or Stanford being private (although public universities, including world-class Berkeley, account for over 70 per cent of all students there). In most European countries, by contrast, the private sector is less significant and is of lower status than the public one: students typically apply to private institutions having failed to gain entry to more prestigious public ones. As always, there are exceptions to the rule: students may choose a well-regarded denominational university such as the Catholic University of Louvain/Leuven in Belgium, or the Catholic University of Lublin in Poland, in preference to a secular institution. In Europe, in most cases, little research is undertaken in private universities, although prominent exceptions are private business schools such as INSEAD in France and IESE in Spain.

Private universities can be categorized according to the role they play in the relevant national higher education structure. One such typology differentiates them into 'more', 'better', and 'different' categories: that is, they either simply provide more student places not available through the state sector to meet national demands (i.e. 'demand-absorbing' as in, say, Poland or Japan—and in both countries more recently they are facing contraction as demographic change sees fewer 18–25-year-olds seeking to enter higher education); they provide better educational quality than in the state sector (as is the case to some extent in the USA); or they offer a different kind of higher education (focused on a professional career, perhaps, or with a religious orientation).

Britain poses difficulties for international agencies seeking to categorize universities in these terms: on one reckoning, all British universities are private as independent chartered or statutory corporations—they set their own overall policies, their buildings are not owned by the state, their staff are not civil servants but are recruited and employed by the university for which they work on terms set by that university, they decide which students they wish to admit—yet they are strongly affected by government policies, particularly on finance. But most people in Britain would probably think of universities as public rather than private institutions, and with good reason—they do, after all, aim to serve public purposes and have governance structures that emphasize accountability. (As our late colleague David Watson, to whom this book is dedicated, remarked, 'The answer to the question, "Are British universities public or private?" is, "Yes".')

In the US during the 1980s and 1990s the for-profit sector expanded hugely (the University of Phoenix now has some 300,000 students, and its owner paid $600 million for BPP

University in the UK—which it has since sold on again for supposedly $900 million), building on the historic presence of proprietary or trade schools; and such *minban* have also helped China cope with its on-going process of recent, very rapid massification to over thirty million students. A similar story applies following the 1989 revolutions in several Eastern European countries and in parts of Latin America—for instance, over 70 per cent of students are enrolled at private universities in Brazil and in Chile; and some 20 per cent are in for-profits within Brazil. Such for-profit providers typically focus on skills- and competencies-based vocational degrees in fields such as management, accountancy, law, and marketing—rather than expensive-to-teach subjects such as the sciences and engineering, or those such as philosophy where students do not see an obvious link to getting jobs. They prefer economical, standardized teaching, deploying few resources, to chasing the kudos of research or entering the so-called 'arms-race' of glitzy campus infrastructure. In the US, these for-profits have often developed from being trade schools to now serving neglected, disadvantaged groups where there has been a lack of capacity in the public community colleges (higher education delivered within the further education sector in other countries). However, there has been recent political controversy over: the low completion rates at these US for-profits; the loan debts their students incur; the disproportionate amount these businesses spend on marketing rather than teaching; and very recently there have been some spectacular insolvencies. In some countries these for-profit higher education providers are seen by government as something to encourage as a means of injecting new competition into the sector, thereby engendering both pedagogical innovation (for instance, digital learning or year-long teaching for shorter and less costly degree courses) and also price/fees competition.

In many ways, a more important distinction than between public or private is whether the institution is operated as a for-profit or non-profit entity. The for-profit private sector in the US—as distinct from the non-profit private universities—has acquired a poor reputation in recent years, recruiting significantly from underqualified applicants able to gain access to federal government student aid programmes, but providing them in some cases with sub-standard education in return for handsome profits. The recent rapid growth of for-profit institutions in Britain has raised similar questions about the use of public funds to subsidize low-standard provision (though in Britain, many for-profit institutions also rely on fee-paying students from outside the EU). The for- and non-profit distinction is not necessarily hard-and-fast, however: an ostensibly non-profit, private institution may be owned by a for-profit company, from which it is required to buy services, thus transferring revenue to the for-profit entity. Recently, some British for-profit higher education institutions, operating mainly in fields where costs are low and fees high, such as law and accountancy, have obtained degree-awarding powers; previously, their degrees were validated by public universities. This apparently technical change has opened a debate about what it means, or should mean, to be a 'real' university. Can an enterprise whose primary purpose is to make profits for its shareholders be considered to be a university if it may close or change ownership should it fail to deliver the profits its owners expect? Can it be a university if it operates only in a few areas of applied work, with no significant commitment to knowledge production? Can it be a university if it has minimal commitment to the wider society in which it works? It remains to be seen whether for-profit universities become a developing trend in Britain or whether they will continue to play only a marginal role in the wider higher education landscape.

The state and the university

The relationship between the state and the university has already been mentioned. This is a crucial relationship everywhere. For the modern state, the university has a key role in advanced training, scientific and technical research, the preservation of national cultural resources, and probably other policy areas such as regional development and social mobility. For the university, whether public or private, the state is a source of income (which may include meeting all or some of the costs of teaching, and research grants and contracts) and also a guarantor of university freedoms and powers: the state may limit the number of institutions that can award degrees, for example, thus giving quasi-monopoly powers to existing institutions by erecting entry barriers to protect them.

Across the world—most countries in Europe, Asia, Africa, Australasia, and Latin America—universities were typically established as state institutions, though often with some recognition of the desirability of academic freedom. This meant that local decision-making was usually very limited, as staff and student numbers were probably centrally determined, and with university budgets prescribed in detail by the relevant government department. As higher education has expanded globally from the later decades of the 20th century and as international comparisons have become more significant, this strongly centralized approach has come in for criticism: the European Commission, for example, has argued that tight state control prevents universities from responding readily to changing needs and thus making their fullest contribution to economic development and social cohesion. This has led to a shift in thinking, from a state control model to one of 'state steering', with the state authority setting general objectives and financial limits, but leaving it to individual university managements to determine local priorities and policies. Although an apparently simple change, it can be hard to put into practice in a system with entrenched ways of working, and where a change of this sort may shift the balance of power against established interests. Governments everywhere, however, tend to be reluctant to surrender fully the influence offered by at least some direct control over university affairs.

International convergence

We have noted the fundamental similarity of universities, regardless of nationalities, and a convergence towards a single university model in terms of its broad academic and organizational frameworks. Nobody at present is making serious claims for a completely new type of university, although experiments continue with various methods of teaching and learning: distance learning using the Internet, for example. These new methods, though, are essentially ways of widening access to more-or-less traditional institutions and the academic resources that they possess. MOOCs are another example, allowing anyone in the world with an interest in a particular topic and an Internet connection to take part in a free online course offered by a university (though gaining accreditation in the form of transferable credits for learning may involve a charge). None of these developments, however, has apparently reduced the attraction of an established university with a good academic reputation and an attractive physical campus or city location: students continue to travel across the world to seek them out. Indeed, universities are increasingly realizing the need to support the social, face-to-face aspects of learning, by physical improvements to their campuses (the university as 'country club'), creating more flexible teaching spaces, and informal learning and social spaces. There is now, arguably, more emphasis on improving the way the face-to-face university works (emphasizing the 'student experience') than there is on developing distance modes of teaching and learning. Ideas that were current around the turn of the century for 'unbundling' universities (breaking up existing university structures so that centralized, and hopefully lower cost, administrative functions could serve different groups of teachers and researchers in different locations) or the creation of genuinely multinational universities (campuses in different countries teaching to a common pattern under centralized management) seem to have faded away.

We discuss in Chapter 4 the growth of university league tables of various kinds: while these certainly have major methodological drawbacks, they have had the effect of focusing the attention of university managements and national authorities on how other universities operate. This has not surprisingly led to attempts at emulation of the more highly ranked institutions and systems—a process which has shown how difficult it is to make dramatic improvements in relative standings of institutions, when everyone else is also trying to make similar improvements.

One approach to international convergence is the Bologna Process (mentioned in Chapter 2). This began with a declaration by the education ministers of twenty-nine European countries in 1999 to harmonize their higher education systems. There are currently forty-seven participating countries, which collectively make up the European Higher Education Area (EHEA)—which now stretches well beyond Europe. The basic idea here is to make the structures of university programmes more similar and (crucially) credit-based, so that students can more easily undertake study in different countries, taking their credits with them. The Bologna Process requires signatory countries to move towards a so-called '3+2+3' structure: a three- (or four-)year Bachelor's degree (often described as 'short cycle' because many countries had much longer first-degree programmes), perhaps followed by a two-year Master's course, with some students going on to a three-year Doctoral programme (with longer periods applying for part-time study). Some signatory countries were glad to have the opportunity offered by Bologna to re-structure their higher education systems to try to improve efficiency. In some cases, conservatism in universities—and, it is believed, that of employers, wary of unfamiliar degree offerings—has made changes to structures more apparent than real: for example, leaving it still as a standard practice to take a Master's degree immediately after a first degree, so making the first 'cycle' effectively five or six years and losing the flexibility which Bologna was intended to encourage.

Even so, the Bologna Process has been remarkable in that so many countries have wished to join it, even those such as Russia with long-established traditions rather different to those underlying the Bologna policies. It has created a momentum for change, even if the Bologna website shows that progress in many member states has been somewhat limited. This takes us back to our earlier point about the similarities between universities across countries which otherwise have rather little in common: governments seem to have recognized that the exclusion of their own universities from this EHEA trans-national process would somehow count against them.

Some interesting data about the size and shape of different higher education systems

Finally, in this chapter on the global patterns of higher education, some data on different national systems...

The UK

Here is a 2015 snapshot of the size and shape of one major higher education system where about 40 per cent of those aged 18–19 now enter university; there are some 2.3 million students spread across c.160 higher education providers; these institutions have a total income of around £30 billion, and employ some 190,000 academics; within the 2.3 million students 1.75 million are undergraduates and half of the 2.3 million are concentrated into just the five subject areas of business, health, social studies, biological sciences, and education; one in eight undergraduates are from overseas and four in ten on graduate courses are international students, the biggest source of such non-UK students being EU countries at 30 per cent (with students from Germany representing the largest group), followed by China (20 per cent) and the rest of Asia (another 20 per cent); the fee-income from these c.310,000 non-UK/EU students is just under £4 billion. The UK spends 1.8 per cent of its GDP on higher education compared to, for example, almost 3 per cent in the US (20 million students); 2.5 per cent each in Canada and Korea; c.1.75 per cent in the Netherlands and the Nordic countries; c.1.5 per cent each for Australia, Japan, and France; c.1.25 per cent each in Germany (3 million students), Switzerland, and Poland; 1 per cent each in Italy and Hungary; and under 1 per cent in Brazil (8 million students). The UK has a thoroughly international student mix making up 15 per cent of undergraduates, 49 per cent of Master's students, 44 per cent of PhD students. (Australia is similar with an equivalent split of 30/56/36, respectively, while the US is less so with a split of 3/11/27, respectively; Germany is even less so at 3/10/15 as is Japan at 2.5/9/19.) Research is highly concentrated, as in the USA, in the elite end of the 160 or so UK universities—for example, within England the Higher Education Funding Council in 2017/18 handed out $c.$£1.6 billion for supporting research, of which: almost a fifth went to Oxford and Cambridge alone; over a third went to Oxbridge plus the major London institutions of University College, King's, and Imperial; and over half went to these five plus the next seven largest recipients (while, in contrast, a collective of another dozen universities received barely half of 1 per cent of that £1.6 billion!).

The brief Golden Age during the 1950s and 1960s of generous public funding for higher education as a free public good began to end in the UK by the mid-1970s (and a little later in the US and in the rest of Europe)—for instance, the taxpayer annual subsidy per undergraduate fell away by well over a third from 1980 to 2000 (then tuition fees were introduced for English universities, first at £1,000 per annum (pa); then £3,000 pa; to the current £9,250 pa); in the US over the same decades the states' funding per student dropped by around a third while fees doubled; and in the Netherlands, for example, since 2000 the number of students has risen by about 100,000 to just over 250,000 while the government grant to universities per student has fallen by around a quarter. England now has perhaps the highest tuition fees globally outside of the USA's prestigious, private non-profits such as Stanford and Harvard. However, its very sophisticated 'income-contingent' loans scheme (covering both fees and living costs) is fairer than in many countries, so that young people from all socio-economic groups do not appear to have been deterred from 'going to uni' despite these high fees. However, as in almost all countries, a persistent gap remains in terms of the children of higher socio-economic strata being far more likely to attend university (making free higher education for all a regressive blanket benefit for the well-off in society). The loans-debt burden for graduates in the UK is heavy because in part it covers living away from the parental home (some 80% of UK students live away from home compared to, for instance, only 25% in Italy, 40% in France, and 50% in Spain).

The US

Taking a glance at the US system, the percentage of the cohort aged 25–9 who had been to college was barely 5 per cent in 1950, was still only some 10 per cent by 1970, but had surged to around 30 per cent in 2010. In 1950, 70 per cent of students were male; by 2010 just under 60 per cent were female. Student debt topped $1.2 trillion in 2015, the cost of 'going to college' as part of the American Dream (ushered in by the GI Bill, aka the Serviceman's Readjustment Act 1944, expanding US higher education: some 2.25 million military 'veterans' attended college over the next decade) having increased by a factor of ten (after adjusting for inflation) compared to the 1950s, and even outpacing the inflation in US medical costs—with much of the increasingly perceived unaffordability resulting from states reducing their grants for public higher education institutions over the past decade (some public universities now get less than 10 per cent of their budget by way of their state funding). In the top quartile of household income distribution over 75 per cent of the family's children enter higher education; it is not quite 10 per cent for the lowest quartile. About 80 per cent of children from families in the top quintile by income gain a first degree, while by the fourth quintile it is under 20 per cent, and it is less than 10 per cent for the lowest quintile. The alleged 'under-employment' (or 'over-education') of graduates is estimated at over one-third.

The US has more than 4,000 higher education institutions, with only just over 100 being research-focused universities and a further 450 or so grant research-based PhDs; about 1,450 are commercial for-profit operations (the 1979 comparable figures were 3,125 and just 100; having expanded hugely, more recently their numbers have contracted). In 1979, 29 per cent of the 1.5 million or so faculty were full-time tenured and 24 per cent were part-time casuals or adjuncts; by 2013, the figures were 17 per cent and 43 per cent. The Federal government spends over $65 billion on research in US universities, with 40 per cent going to just thirty institutions. Stanford has earned some $1.3 billion in royalties from over 8,000 inventions and sold its Google stock for $336 million—other Stanford spin-offs include LinkedIn, Netflix, and eBay. The University has thirty-eight Nobel Laureates and an endowment of over $20 billion; but Harvard has twice as many Nobel Prizes and an endowment almost double that of Stanford. Yale has an endowment of c.$24 billion; Princeton, $21 billion; Massachusetts Institute of Technology (MIT), $12.5 billion. Michigan, with the largest public university endowment, is under $10 billion (Oxford and Cambridge each struggle to get much above $7.5 billion).

China

In China, the number of higher education institutions has increased from about 1,000 in 1990 to 2,725 or so by 2010, with the number of undergraduate students jumping from two million to over thirty million during these thirty years—indeed, the annual growth rate topped 35 per cent in each of the years 1999 and 2000. Now over 25 per cent of the 18–21 cohort enter higher education. China's Project

211 and Project 985 excellence initiatives have selectively funded research at certain universities (notably Peking, Fudan, and Tsinghua as China's MIT), propelling forty-four into the top 500 ranked by research output globally compared to fourteen in 2004 (the US equivalent figures over that decade show a drop from 170 to 146, with falls in the UK from forty-two to thirty-eight; in Germany from forty-three to thirty-nine; and in Japan from thirty-six to nineteen).

Globally

The GTER (gross tertiary enrolment rate) in HPs (high participation systems) trebled from an average of 10 per cent in 1972 to 32 per cent by 2012, but there were GTERs of 50 per cent or more in some fifty-four HPs and even over 75 per cent in fourteen. The percentage of those aged 25–34 with a first degree taken over three or more years is some 30 per cent across OECD nations, with the US at 34 per cent (plus another 10 per cent with an associate two-year degree), the UK at 40 per cent, Australia at 37 per cent, France at 27 per cent, Japan at 35 per cent, and Germany at 19 per cent. Universities vary hugely in size, and the world-class elites are generally small—Oxford and Cambridge each have *c.*20,000 students; MIT, barely 11,000; Harvard, 20,000; and Stanford, some 16,500; China's Tsinghua and Peking each have around 30,000. Berkeley is probably the largest, global top-ten, research university with some 40,000 students. Manchester is the UK's largest university with *c.*40,000 students; a large US state university such as Arizona State has something like 80,000. Typically, universities across the world have 50,000–75,000 students, but there are outliers such as Mumbai University with over 550,000; the University of Buenos Aires with 325,000; the National University of Mexico with 225,000; Delhi University with over 130,000; and Rome University with about 112,500.

Chapter 4
How universities and colleges work

As we have noted, the university has evolved from its initial creation in medieval Europe and has spread around the globe. In essence, we now see several variants of the organizational format of the university (as explored in Chapter 3)—and, alongside doom-laden lamentations about 'crisis' (harking back to the supposed halcyon days of universities, which are usually deemed to have been when they were generously funded by the state in the 1960s providing higher education as a free public good), we hear talk of an exciting new form for the university needed to meet the challenges of this new century and arising from disruptive innovation that calls for a radical overhaul of its governance and management structures. The traditionally dominant group in the idea and ideal of the university—the academics or faculty—feel especially threatened by such change, actual and proposed, as they see it amounting to their consensus decision-making based on 'collegiality' or 'shared values' being undermined in the name of economy and efficiency. At its extreme members of faculty see their influence being diluted by a growing cadre of professional management—an expansion sometimes referred to as 'administrative bloat'. On the other hand, the increasing complexity of the modern university and the growth of external regulation can be used with some justification to explain at least part of this expansion of university management numbers and cost.

But, all that noted, the university everywhere continues to be dominated at its core by its teaching activity, of undergraduates for first degrees and of graduates for taught Master's or research degrees. And that teaching is organized in a way that would still look familiar to the university teacher at a medieval university—academic subjects and departments, faculties based on collectives of them, staff hierarchy from professor down, the pattern of the academic year, lectures, reading lists, examinations, degree classifications, graduation ceremonies with gowns and mortar-boards/caps, maces, degree scrolls, and so on.

Besides teaching and research, many universities will lay claim to a third leg of desirable activity by way of their contribution through consultancy and the exploitation of intellectual property to their local economy (there will be stress on being 'the entrepreneurial university'), and also by their pursuing 'civic engagement' in seeking to address social issues of various kinds (all this activity is often referred to as 'service' in a US context). Sometimes governments will fund this extra activity by universities as a means of stimulating regional development, a source of taxpayer finance on top of whatever is also supplied for teaching or for research. Governments also like the idea of universities contributing to 'the knowledge economy', or even 'the knowledge society', as they seek a competitive edge for the nation within a globalized economy. But in recent decades there has been taxpayer retreat from the once lavish funding of higher education and hence 'privatization' of universities in the sense that the traditional public-sector institutions have sought other sources of income beyond dependence on public funding. This process of change brings with it (often resented) ideas of the 'commercialization' and 'commodification' of the university, of its 'marketization' through increased competition for funds (including from fee-paying students) and of 'managerialism' and 'corporatism' as institutions are said to need tighter top–down control to operate in this harsher financial environment. Much of this is also true, of course, for other areas of what was once exclusively public-sector economic activity and services, driven by the modern (allegedly 'neoliberal') zeitgeist of 'new public management' and by a search for 'accountability' based on the extensive use of 'performance indicators' or 'metrics'.

Thus, what was once benign 'state funding' of the university in the middle of the 20th century in most countries became increased 'state control' through such accountability for this funding. More recently in some countries, as taxpayer financing of higher education gives way to the student paying tuition fees we see the 'state steering' rather than the state funding of higher education—with the related concept that, for example, the US state or regional public university has moved from being *state funded* through being *state assisted* to, in some cases, arguably, being merely *state located* (as direct public funding has fallen to less than 10 per cent of total income)—some even complain of now being *state impeded*! The conundrum is whether the gradual reduction in government funding actually leaves the university with increased autonomy, and whether the university welcomes such a change as providing an opportunity to gain control of its strategic destiny or whether it fears this change as representing a threat in having to make its way without instructions from the Ministry of Education.

The issue is complicated to some degree by the legal jurisdiction within which the university operates. The English common law tradition operating in the UK, Australia, New Zealand, Canada, and the US (excluding state/public universities) sees the university as an independent, private, charitable corporation, albeit one that may have developed a degree of dependency on government grants—as such, the university is allowed to manage itself as it sees fit until or unless the law is altered to prevent it doing so. In contrast, the civil code nations of continental Europe, Latin America, and much of Asia usually view the university as an emanation of the central state, as a public entity with its academics as civil servants, and hence new higher education laws are needed in order to deregulate the universities—the university can do only what it is allowed to do.

Universities are in some nations seen as broadly equal, so that students simply and conveniently attend their local institution—just as they might have gone to their neighbourhood state school. In other countries, universities form an increasingly stratified hierarchy or pyramid of institutions, based on the easily measured research output for the top/elite branded universities or based on their (very much more difficult to measure) teaching quality that is assumed to link to the employability of their graduates. The emergence of influential worldwide rankings (measuring perhaps 1,000 out of approaching 20,000 universities and colleges globally) over the past decade or so has driven a scramble for strategic repositioning, usually by diverting resources towards the pursuit of the cash and kudos of research, and often at the neglect of adequately resourcing undergraduate teaching. In some countries, the government has even injected extra funds into carefully selected universities hoping to get a top-fifty or top-twenty institution by a specified point in the future. The rankings tend to be dominated by a premier league of ten 'world-class' super-research universities—with Berkeley, Cambridge, Harvard, Imperial College London, MIT, Oxford, Princeton, Stanford, University College London, and Yale all jostling for inclusion in a top-ten currently taken up exclusively by these US and UK institutions. Further down the hierarchy, a few Asian universities (Tokyo, National University Singapore, Hong Kong University (Figure 5), and especially in China Tsinghua and Peking) are climbing rapidly, usually as a result of heavily increased government funding for carefully selected institutions. There is, however, an appropriate debate as to whether it is better for governments to fund a world-class higher education *nation-wide* system rather than spending money on just a few institutions in what is a costly, zero-sum game in terms of vying for a place in a strictly limited top-fifty, for example, or on some other costly, macho (perhaps unrealistic) policy ambition.

In considering how universities work it is helpful to ask who 'owns' the university (Figure 6). Originally there was not much to own with it being a loose collection or guild of teaching Masters

5. Hong Kong Polytechnic University, Innovation Tower (2013; by Zaha Hadid)—an example of the famous-name-architect, bold, exciting architecture ('starchitecture') increasingly found in the 21st-century university, the building's style announcing the innovative academic work going on inside. Asian universities are setting the pace in many fields.

gathering in fee-paying students to lecture to in rented rooms at Paris or Oxford University in 1250—it might possess a ceremonial mace (Figure 6), later a library of books, and perhaps some buildings for lectures, examinations, and meetings. Now it is a massive business with a huge infrastructure of laboratories, teaching spaces, offices, libraries, residence blocks, sports centres, catering outlets, shops, committee rooms, and car-parks. After the cost of salaries, at over half of total spend, the next biggest expense is on premises, at 15–20 per cent, especially where there is an 'arms race' to build glitzier learning spaces or student recreational facilities

6. The university mace—the symbol (based on medieval weaponry!) of the medieval academic guild's status as a corporate body, as also for, say, a municipal council or a London livery company, with the academic robes signifying the distinctions gained by their wearers.

than those offered at competitor institutions; the unsuspecting applicant/customer, finding it hard to evaluate teaching quality, hence uses the appearance of the campus (and the high fees!) as a proxy guide for what he or she hopes will be 'a good university'.

The medieval gathering of Masters did soon form 'the university' as a corporation or with some similar legal status, but worldwide today only at Oxford, Cambridge, and Trinity College Dublin is this guild of academics ('dons') still constitutionally sovereign. Elsewhere the modern university is ultimately controlled either by a lay-dominated board/council or by a governmental higher education authority. The more research-focused the university, the more likely it is that the voice of the academics or faculty will be influential in its governance and management, via a senate or academic board. Thus, the university is in most cases 'owned' (in trust) by its corporate body, but sometimes directly by the central or regional government.

Box 6. On university power politics, 1930s style

C.P. Snow, in *The Masters* (1951), provides a novel about academic power politics and the competing candidates (Jago v. Crawford) in the 1930s election of the head of a self-governing Cambridge college. This gives us the most famous picture of how Oxford and Cambridge 'dons' supposedly behave within their cloistered and confined world, and it is still routinely (re-)read as Oxbridge Fellows prepare to find themselves a new Head of House as 'first among equals' within the fellowship—sadly, modern elections are usually rather more mundane than in *The Masters*:

> On the morning of the election.... The Chapel door stood open, and the head porter, his top hat gleaming in the grey morning, was waiting to give the signal for the bell to peal.... The bell rang out insistently.... A long table had been placed in the nave; it was covered with a thick rich crimson table-cloth.... The bell gave its last peal: the chimes of ten were quivering above the Chapel.... In front of each of us, on the crimson cloth, was a copy of the statutes, a slip of paper, and a pen. Down the middle of the table ran a series of four inkstands.... [The Fellows vote, and Crawford is elected Master] Without a word, Jago leaned across the table, shook Crawford's hand, and walked out of the Chapel. Everyone watched him go. It was not until the outer door swung to that chairs were pushed back and men surrounded Crawford. We congratulated him.... It was strange to hear him for the first time called Master...

(That said, the Fellows of New College, Oxford, continued for the 2015 election of a Warden the tradition of processing, be-gowned, into and then being locked inside their medieval chapel by the bowler-hatted head porter while they voted, with an accompanying peal of bells once they had reached a result.)

Is there corruption in the governance and management of universities? Yes, as in any and all organizations run by people and involving the moving around of money. In most countries such risk of corruption will be very low; in others there will indeed be bribes paid to get university places, to pass exams, even to gain employment. Sometimes the corruption will take the form of nepotism, cronyism, or clientelism—jobs and promotions for family members, for friends, or for members of a particular group or political party. And everywhere there is a growing problem—aided by the Internet and the ability to pay somebody through 'essay mills' to write assignments—of students cheating and plagiarizing. Even in some otherwise relatively corruption-free nations like the US there is what some would see as corruption by way of lower entry grades for the children of donors (who usually are also alumni of the university concerned)—these are 'legacy candidates'. And occasionally there are scandals over grades or marks allegedly being interfered with by 'management' to ensure that international students paying lucratively high tuition fees are able to continue their academic studies. Again, even in the US and in the UK or Australia, there have been scandals over cheating by academics in their research methods or in claiming credit for the break-throughs achieved by junior colleagues. And, there are, sadly, entire entities called 'university' that are utterly corrupt—they are scam entities known as 'degree mills' that sell bogus qualifications, often, of course, bought by equally corrupt folk hoping they will convince a potential employer; but sometimes such fake universities are used to enable pretend students to get through immigration into a country and the entity then also benefits from the 'students' being able to draw down government loan monies to pay its fees.

With respect to US higher education two other unique features, beyond the special concept of 'legacy candidates' mentioned earlier, that also create controversy as well as difficult management problems are 'intercollegiate athletics' and 'fraternities' (the matching sororities rarely grab the headlines). Some argue that the vast cost of college quasi-professional football (with the coach commonly being the most well-paid employee on campus) distorts the academic mission (starting with admitting academically underqualified athletes and then nursing them to some sort of degree result) and also the institution's finances (only a few such programmes generate a real surplus to subsidize academic activity as the prime purpose of the university or college). But, given the strong alumni commitment to the fraternity system (the so-called 'Greeks' because they are named by the letters of the Greek alphabet) and also to university athletics, it is hard for the administration to question the funding of football just as it is to try and close down fraternity houses after yet another 'hazing' incident causes the tragic death or maiming of a male student, or after another episode of sexual aggression towards female students.

Finally, in terms of this broad flagging of governance and management issues in how universities function, is the university some special, some exceptional organization that needs to be governed and managed differently to all others? Some would very strongly argue, 'Yes': it must be controlled only by those who fully understand what academic life is about; ideally it should be run by the professors for the professors if it is to fulfil its duty of preserving, enhancing, and disseminating knowledge, of serving culture and civilization, of speaking truth to power. Thus, they would claim, those professors must be protected from crude, short-term, ignorant, arrogant, non-academic managers; and they must have life-long job security ('tenure') against dismissal for saying what the powerful may not want to hear ('academic freedom') within the context of 'university autonomy'. 'Nonsense', say others: the university has always existed to serve somebody more powerful, somebody with money to fund the scholars—the medieval church or monarch, latterly the modern state; and indeed nowadays to serve its fee-paying student customers, just like any other business supplying a service to consumers. Thus, they would assert, it needs to be fully accountable, properly governed, efficiently managed by professional managers not amateurs who take too long to reach a consensus about urgent pressure for change or who refuse to face up to difficult issues.

So, the age-old and endless discussion continues. What is the balance of managerialism v. collegiality, of corporatism v. shared values? Are the professors simply hired labour in gowns, or do they have some special ownership of the enterprise which is just empty infrastructure without their learning? The treatment of the faculty will vary according to their mobility—those that can readily get a post at another elite university will 'walk' if treated badly by University X, so, arguably, the top-fifty or so world-class, research-led universities have very similar human resource policies for their academic staff. But, down the hierarchy, probably the professor is less independent and more managed than in the past—and many will complain that the student consumer empowered as a fee-paying customer in many countries over recent years is now less deferential and more demanding of professors being professional.

Universities vary greatly as to what is the balance of actual power or influence as opposed to the formal constitutional position within the triangle of academic staff as the faculty, managers as the executive, and lay members as the trustees. In theory, absolute power formally lies with the council or board, but subject to close working with the senate or academic board on academic issues. As noted earlier, the more research-focused the university (say, for example, the barely 100 of the very many higher education institutions in the US, and perhaps twenty-five of the UK's roughly 150), the greater the influence of the faculty—and, conversely, the more teaching-focused the university, the more likely that it is to be corporatist and top–down managed by a powerful executive. Why is this? Partly because top researchers demand greater autonomy over their working conditions and can readily find another post if their present one does not suit them. And partly because teaching-only universities need to manage large flows of students and to teach them to consistent standards, which requires standardized processes and leads to less autonomy for those teaching them.

Much of the debate about reshaping the university for this century to be more market-responsive (not least in managing—if not outright manipulating—the metrics that dictate the institution's performance and position in the variety of league tables) is about adjusting the balance within the triangle of governance, and usually to the disadvantage of the professoriate (which some see as being proletarianized—downgraded to just another section of the workforce). Within the governance triangle, only relatively rarely is there a formal governance place for more than a token representation of students or of non-academic employees (still less of alumni as another stakeholder group). Tensions arise within this triangle of organizational interactions, typically, when the governors as trustees get the balance wrong between holding the executive to account and yet not micro-managing; when the faculty recognize an incompetent executive but the trustees ignore the complaints from the academics; or when faculty's unreasonable and selfish resistance to necessary change is allowed by the trustees to trump sensible proposals from the executive.

The university must effectively administer, if not indeed manage, the delivery of teaching (and associated examining and assessment) as well as, in some cases, the organization of research—plus third-leg consultancy and civic engagement activity as part of the contribution of the university to regional development and, along with its output of (hopefully) skilled and employable graduates, to 'the knowledge economy'. The number and the cost of the administrative staff involved have grown hugely over recent decades and these staff are increasingly specialized, focusing on teaching and learning, quality audit, research services and intellectual property exploitation, HR, PR, diversity and equality, IT, estates, security (US campuses often employ their own police force—with guns!), finance, development and alumni relations, student financial aid, international collaborations and cross-border partnerships, overseas student recruitment, marketing, strategic planning, legal services, counselling, accommodation, etc., etc. Critics often assert that the finance function is particularly underdeveloped in the not-for-profit university compared to the for-profit university and other commercial organizations, with a poor understanding of what drives cost and with weak cost control (especially of capital IT or buildings projects): leading to the steady hiking of tuition fees where the national politics of higher education allow freedom for universities to control their fees/prices. The cost of administration/management has increased dramatically over recent decades, partly it is argued (in defence of the bureaucrats) because more are needed to ensure the university can comply with ever-greater external regulation, and so the administration budget can now easily exceed 10 per cent of total institutional spend—with critics declaring that presidents or vice-chancellors are rather overpaid.

Academics in turn often claim that a proliferation of allegedly second-rate managers spend their time trying out the failed fads of yesterday's management techniques, bombarding professors with jargon and acronym-filled memos about the latest initiative on responsibility-centred management, performance budgeting, zero-based budgets, overhead recovery, performance measurement of teaching quality and productivity or of research output. Certainly in most countries vast amounts of data are now routinely collected via detailed surveys, usually triggered nationally in the name of accountability and value-for-money in relation to taxpayer inputs—but it is often unclear the degree to which policy-making in higher education thereby becomes evidence-based and hence supposedly better. And while research productivity can be monitored with some precision on the basis of counting the publications of academics and then the citation of them in academic journals by other academics, the meaningful measurement of teaching quality by university management or by national quality and standards agencies remains elusive.

This is because there is considerable fuzziness over just what is indeed 'higher' about higher education; about what is the standard of 'graduateness' and whether it is consistent within and across universities, let alone countries; over how to define and monitor quality in higher education teaching—as opposed, more easily, to measuring the quantum of teaching offered within a degree course (by way, say, of the number of lectures, the size of seminar groups, the frequency of assignments and the speed of giving feedback on the student's performance in them). And is teaching quality to be left to the professional integrity of the faculty (perhaps distracted by the delights and rewards of research as the key factor in academic reputations and promotions), or to be set by the governors and enforced by an internal management hierarchy (Box 7), or regulated by some external agency, or indeed demanded by the empowered fee-paying student consumer? Countries constantly experiment with costly bureaucratic regimes of quality audit; and to an extent the professional bodies in medicine, engineering, pharmacy, and similar help to maintain standards in some subject areas where gaining the degree also admits the person to membership of a professional body as a licence to practise. But beyond such disciplines there is said to be a steady decline in at least the teaching quantum, leading arguably to lower standards of 'graduateness' and perhaps made worse by grade inflation arising from lenient marking by academics being graded themselves in student satisfaction surveys used as metrics by managers. And internal university management, some allege, appears to ignore if not actually condone this deterioration.

Yet, if not this cadre of unloved professional managers, who else can prepare the university for the 'disruptive change' that is seen to be looming in the delivery of higher education? Change coming, for instance, by way of increased competition from possible new entrants in the form of the for-profit providers; of new technology for digital and distance learning, not least the use of MOOCs (see Chapter 3) that could, some say, replace the bricks and mortar campus with clicks—far more cheaply and

Box 7. On university power politics, 1900s style

Less well-known than Snow (Box 6) or Bradbury (Box 9) is
F.M. Cornford (*Microcosmographia Academica: Being a Guide for
the Young Academic Politician*, 1908) as an account of old-style
university politics (still operative in some institutions); here
on the art of prevarication and delay in university (non-)
decision-making.

> When other methods of obstruction fail, you should have
> recourse to Wasting Time; for, although it is recognised
> in academic circles that time in general is of no value,
> considerable importance is attached to teatime, and by
> deferring this, you may exasperate any body of men to the
> point of voting against anything. The simplest method is
> Boring. Talk slowly and indistinctly, at a little distance
> from the point....Another sport which wastes unlimited
> time is Comma-hunting...

Charles W. Eliot, former President of Harvard University for
forty years, on retirement wrote the first comprehensive book on
university governance and management (*University Administration*,
1908) and in addressing the politics of and the power balance
within the governance triangle (the governors as the governing
body—the executive as the administration—the faculty as the
senate) noted that the lay, non-expert governing body

> ordinarily follows the advice of the [expert] university
> faculties [since it is rightly] the common custom for
> trustees to consign to the faculties...the immediate
> supervision of the conditions of the academic life
> [since an] experienced band of university trustees will
> always maintain a considerate and even deferential
> attitude towards the experts they employ as regular
> teachers...[given that] the trustees are not expert in any
> branch of university teaching.

(continued)

Box 7. Continued

In some US states the governors/trustees have recently become somewhat distrustful of their expert faculty, while in the UK over the past couple of decades there has been a swing back towards the firm, lay governor, formal authority of the 1900s as the time when the civic universities were created and away from the peak of donnish dominion in the 1960s.

even more effectively delivering learning and credentials (although, alternatively, they might just be absorbed into, indeed neutralized by, the traditional incumbent producer-oriented players); of adverse demographics where a particular nation has a declining proportion of university-age population; of government austerity in funding higher education as a weak competitor to the financing of schools, healthcare, pensions, etc.; of growing competition from other countries for the lucrative global market in high-fees international students.... Thus, the nature and style of the administration both reflects and alters the underlying organizational culture of the university itself. Should it be governed and managed along collegial lines; as a bureaucratic machine; as a command and control corporatist entity; as an enterprising and entrepreneurial venture; or, indeed, as a mix of any and all of these ways—with admissions and exams as bureaucratic mechanisms; teaching as collegial; research resourcing and income-generation from new projects as entrepreneurial; and capital spend as corporatist?

In short, universities are complex operations with complicated workings, trying to fulfil a multitude of (potentially conflicting) tasks and expectations, with a wide variety of demanding stakeholders—suffering from sometimes byzantine governance structures, facing an articulate and vociferous faculty not always entirely engaged with the corporate mission, called upon to solve society's problems while also being accused of being part of this problem, supposed to serve a student customer who may not readily be able to ascertain what he or she really wants from higher education (the theme of Chapter 5). They are not easy to manage; as has sometimes been remarked, they work in practice but not in theory. And, as noted in Box 7, it is not always clear who governs and manages the university: a perplexed new governor-trustee of a US university in the 1950s wrote to his fellow trustees: 'This is a funny kind of business! The specific persons responsible, the Trustees, cannot supervise or manage what is the essence of the business: the educational process itself...'. We will return in Chapter 6 to the issue of managing academics as the professionals delivering the teaching and research missions of the university or college.

Chapter 5
Students: getting in, getting on, getting out

Students: who are they?

Universities are, overwhelmingly, about students—mostly those taking first (Bachelor's) degrees, but also graduates studying for Master's degrees or undertaking research training, perhaps culminating in a PhD. In many countries—certainly in Britain—media commentary and political debate could lead you to assume that 'student' means an 18–21-year-old, studying full-time, straight after leaving school, and leading a student lifestyle—carefree and hedonistic. While it is true that in Britain full-time undergraduates make up the largest single group of students, over a quarter of all students are studying part-time and another quarter are postgraduates (some are both). In both these two categories, many students are older, often starting or coming back to study while working. And 18 per cent of them normally live outside Britain (2012/13 figures). In the US, some 38 per cent of all university students are part-time while 14 per cent are studying for postgraduate degrees (2012 figures). So we need to be careful when speaking of a 'typical' student—in most countries, they are a pretty diverse group, with varying aspirations. Older students, in particular, are often less interested in the social aspects of university life: they are at university to gain a work-related qualification (not all of them, of course) rather than to develop as an individual (or to go to wild parties). Going to university in order to obtain a qualification that might lead to a good job has been, as we have pointed out, the primary motivation for study since the birth of the European university at the end of the 11th century.

The student journey

First-degree students undertake a 'student journey' that differs in detail between countries but (as with other aspects of the university world) has many features in common. One broad distinction is between systems where a range of subjects is studied leading to later specialization, the liberal arts model prevalent in the US and other countries that have followed its model; and a disciplinary approach, where the focus is on one or two (normally related) disciplines from the start.

Having decided that he or she wants to go to university, much then depends on what the potential student has achieved academically so far and his or her personal circumstances (the two are typically intertwined). In some European countries, graduating from high-school provides a (qualified, often) right to university admission—but not necessarily to a university of the student's choosing. Usually, an applicant with a high level of prior academic achievement will seek admission to a high-status university—though a variety of personal factors may lead them to apply to a less prestigious university that is nearer to home, say, or which offers a particular course that attracts them or that has a distinctive ethos. At the other end of the scale, applicants with only low level prior academic achievements may have to accept what they can get—or (often the better choice) commit themselves to further pre-university study. For the majority of students in between these two extremes, in most cases the application process becomes a matter of deciding which universities are likely to accept them and choosing the one that best meets their personal criteria—which may include subject choice, reputation, location, social life (the 'party campus'), and other matters. This of course assumes a relatively open society with few barriers in terms of personal choice. But in many countries, leaving aside purely academic and financial considerations, there will be restrictions of a political, social, ethnic, or religious nature, which, formally or informally, mean that some individuals will have difficulty gaining admission to their preferred, or to any, university. These countries, to put the matter at its mildest, are accordingly missing opportunities to invest in the human capital available to them.

In almost all countries, a key factor in determining university admission is achievement in school; and, in most countries, the children who generally do best at school are, for a mix of interconnected social and economic factors, from better off families, usually with relatively high social status locally, that are able to endow their children with high socio-cultural capital. This almost inevitably means that the social make-up of university students does not reflect that of the society as a whole. It also means that universities are not selecting applicants on some measure of 'pure' academic ability (however defined) but, at best, selecting among those whose social and school experiences have fitted them for university-level study. Elite universities may be challenged to do more to accept students from a broader socio-economic range. They may respond to these demands by offering scholarships or providing special support for students from disadvantaged backgrounds. But ultimately, as university leaders sometimes point out in exasperation, universities cannot on their own rectify deep-seated inequalities in the societies from which they recruit their students. Politicians, though, often find it easier to blame universities for not 'doing more' rather than seeking to tackle social disadvantage more broadly.

Once accepted by a university, the next stage of the student journey is usually an induction process of some kind. This may be relatively formal, organized by the institution, explaining expectations about academic work and providing practical information about day-to-day life in the university and its city (if it is in one). Or it may happen informally, by individual students working things out for themselves with some help from their peers and more senior students; or, perhaps typically, a bit of both. The social aspects of this process are at least as important as the more formally academic: social networks are important in helping new students to feel that they are fitting in (perhaps by realizing that there are other students feeling just as lost as they do), and this reduces the chances of them dropping out. This induction process, often stretching over an entire week, is appropriately named 'Freshers' Week'. It can be not only hectic but also controversial, where in recent years the programme of activities has, on the one hand, involved too much access to alcohol while, on the other, included compulsory sessions on social behaviour.

The main part of the student journey involves day-to-day work on the academic programme that they have joined, steadily gaining (we may hope) in intellectual understanding about the academic discipline but also with growing self-confidence on matters such as analysing data, presenting complex ideas clearly and persuasively, working to deadlines, communicating effectively with teachers and fellow students—all the skills, in fact, that employers typically say they look for in graduate recruits. For students who joined the university directly from school, these are also years of important personal development (which is one reason why measuring the effects of higher education is so difficult; the technical challenge is to separate the effect of students' ageing from what they are being taught—are they 'smarter' just because they're older or because they have learned 'stuff'?). At the same time, participation in student societies of various sorts may link students into different social networks and allow them to develop new interests. In some American universities, the uniquely American institutions of student-run fraternities and sororities have played this role, though occasionally with the negative consequences described in Tom Wolfe's entertaining novel of American undergraduate life, *I am Charlotte Simmons* (Box 8). A version of the US

7. A modern university library—the medieval university library with its chained books becomes the 21st-century digital 'learning space' (with wi-fi and cappuccinos!).

fraternities and of the Princeton eating clubs is the 'nation' at some Swedish and Finnish universities. Dating back to the 1640s, it provides dining and social facilities for student members, as well as life-long networking; the name 'nation' echoing the 'nations' as the divisions within medieval universities such as Paris and Oxford—these Nordic versions of fraternities, however, seem to have more of a cultural and intellectual dimension than the typical American fraternity.

Towards the end of their period as undergraduates, most students start to think seriously about what should come next: possibly further study, but more likely the first steps towards a career (which of course may involve further study). We think about this in the 'Moving on' section later in this chapter. Recently, in the US and in European countries in particular, students have sought 'intern' experiences with potential employers, sometimes throughout their undergraduate years, in order to make themselves look more attractive to possible employers. In the

82

Box 8. On American student life

Tom Wolfe, in *I am Charlotte Simmons* (2004) as a novel set within an elite Ivy League campus, creates one of the most famous characters in the genre of the campus novel:

Dupont University, the Olympian halls of learning housing the cream of America's youth, the roseate Gothic spires and manicured lawns suffused with tradition . . . Or so it appears to beautiful, brilliant Charlotte Simmons, a sheltered freshman form Sparta, North Carolina, who has come here on a full scholarship. But Charlotte soon learns that for the upper-crust coeds of Dupont, sex, Cool, and kegs trump academic achievement every time . . . [as] Charlotte encounters Dupont's elite—her roommate, Beverly, a fleshy, privileged Brahmin in lusty pursuit of lacrosse players; Jojo Johnson, the only white starting player on Dupont's godlike basketball team; the Young Turk of Saint Ray fraternity, Hoyt Thorpe, whose heady sense of entitlement and social domination . . .

And on fraternity 'Greek' life:

From the front parlour [of the fraternity house] came the sound of 'quarters', a drinking game in which the boys gathered around a table in a circle, more or less, each with a jumbo translucent cup of beer before him. They bounced quarters [coins] on their edges, and tried to make them hop into the other players' cups. If you were successful, your opponent had to tilt his head back and the container up and chugalug all twenty ounces . . . the tables, magnificent old pieces that had been here since the huge Palladian mansion was built before the First World War, were now riddled with dents. It was hard to believe there was once Saint Rays [the name of the

(continued)

Box 8. Continued

fraternity] rich enough and religious enough about the great fraternal chain of being to build such a place and buy such furniture, not merely for themselves...but for generations of Saint Rays to come.

For the US campus novels of an earlier era see: Owen Johnson's (1912) *Stover at Yale* and Scott Fitzgerald's (1920) *This Side of Paradise* on Princeton ('Old Nassau...the pleasantest country club in America'), each institution being noted for its socially exclusive hierarchy of student recreational and dining clubs. Stover gains the ultimate Yale honour—he is 'tapped' for (elected to) membership of the Skull and Bones society and is immediately relieved 'to be no longer an outsider, but back among his own with the stamp of approval on his record'. Fitzgerald describes Princeton's dozen or so eating clubs: 'Ivy, detached and breathlessly aristocratic; Cottage, an impressive melange of brilliant adventurers and well-dressed philanderers; Tiger Inn, broad-shouldered and athletic, vitalised by an honest elaboration of prep-school standards...'. Similarly, Harvard's snobbishness is the theme of John Marquand's (1937) *The Late George Apley*. Oxford colleges at this time also got a bad press in Evelyn Waugh's (1945) *Brideshead Revisited*—and so Oxford, like Princeton, has spent decades living down its fictional image as the playground of a pampered social elite.

In fact, the mid-Victorian Newman idea of the university as idealized in Oxford and its colleges (see Box 4)—as also for US elite institutions from the 1920s—focused on 'character' as a key part of the 'merit' required for admission rather than on pure academic achievement. The university was seen as being about the cultivation of an intellectual and cultural elite, as the preparation of suitable young men for life-long civic leadership (in the case of Oxford, also for administering the British Empire); and the Rhodes Scholarships from the early decades of the 20th century linked Oxford and the Ivy League in terms of sending carefully selected graduates of the latter to the former for a final stage in their processing as the next generation of the Establishment. American elite universities took the search for 'merit' as 'character' to an extreme in selecting the 'chosen few', and in thereby sharing a scarce luxury good between various socio-economic and ethnic groups lobbying for a slice of the privileged pie. Even now they are unusual in global terms in that they have admissions policies that boost applications from athletes useful for competitive teams and also from the children of alumni as 'legacy candidates' benefiting from a form of affirmative action for the already privileged (the alumni having pushed back hard against reforms at universities such as Harvard, Yale, and Princeton that sought to base admission solely on academic achievement—in Oxford and Cambridge the shift since the 1960s towards academic merit as the only determinant of selection was more definitive, as discussed in Box 11).

competitive recruitment context within some countries, universities seek to differentiate themselves by stressing the extent to which they prepare their students for 'employability' as graduates by, say, organizing internships and offering 'entrepreneurship' or 'teamwork skills' as part of the teaching process.

Partners or customers?

The relationship of the individual student to their university is an unusual one. In Western higher education, for a long period, the student was generally viewed by the university authorities and its academic staff as some kind of apprentice to the academic discipline: there to learn, certainly, but not quite in the way a high-school student would learn; rather, to play a supporting role in the knowledge production process and thereby to absorb an understanding of the discipline concerned. Several important features of traditional university life followed from this conception.

One was that students were considered to be members of the university, albeit junior members, with certain rights and responsibilities. The role was neither that of an employee nor that of someone attending merely to master a new skill, as they might be at a technical college in further rather than higher education. Another important feature was that teaching methods, as a school teacher would understand them, were considered less necessary for a university academic to grasp than a deep knowledge of the discipline and a research orientation towards it—with a desire to extend knowledge in that area. Students would, it was tacitly assumed, learn by exposure to this atmosphere of scholarship and research at least as much as by formal, structured teaching. It therefore also followed that students were expected to take a great deal of personal responsibility for their learning, with teaching contact hours (lectures, seminars, tutorials) comprising a small proportion of their time—though students in science and technology subjects usually needed to spend a good deal of time in the laboratory. (Medicine was always different, as students spent a large part of their time in hospitals and usually formed a distinctive community where professional norms typically took precedence over academic ones.)

The traditional relationship between students and their university teachers was, therefore, highly variable, depending on personal inclinations on both sides of the relationship rather than on formal, structured arrangements. When it worked well, with committed teachers and students, both sides derived a great deal of satisfaction from it. Needless to say, there were plenty of examples where it did not work well.

Several things have caused this picture to change in many countries in recent years. One is the expansion of higher education, moving from an elite system to a mass system. Figures for 2014 show that on average for all OECD countries, 33 per cent of adults have undertaken some form of tertiary education (mostly Bachelor's degrees), with eleven countries achieving rates of over 40 per cent.

The figures for almost all of these countries show a rising trend, with younger people having on average received more formal education than older citizens. Higher education systems dealing with nearly half of a country's young adult population need to be designed on different principles to one—as in, say, Britain in the 1960s—that admitted less than 10 per cent of it. (In the academic year preceding the outbreak of the Second World War, there were just 5,093 full-time university teachers in Britain—not enough even to fill a modest-sized football ground—and barely 50,000 students.) Structures in a mass system need to be more formal, with an emphasis on well-organized teaching and learning; for most institutions, a rather informal apprenticeship model is no longer plausible. As expansion has driven up the total cost of higher education, a reaction in many countries has been to reduce the cost per student in an attempt (usually only partially successful) to control overall cost increases: for example, between 1980 and 2000 the number of students in the UK more than doubled while the annual public funding per student pretty well halved. This has added further pressures to formalize and standardize teaching and learning, sometimes with academic posts and workloads linked to student numbers, thus changing profoundly both the nature of the academic job and the relationship of academics to their students.

Expansion and cost increases have led to debates about student tuition fees in many countries. While tuition fees have always been a part of university life in the United States—in public as well as in private universities—the situation has been more varied elsewhere. Traditionally, higher education in continental Europe was an elite enterprise, entirely state-funded, with no fees payable by students who had graduated from high-school. Some European countries (notably Germany and Ireland) have in recent years introduced student fees only to then abandon them. Other European countries levy fees at very low levels. The British position on student fees reflected the anomalous nature of its higher education system. Student fees had been a significant part of universities' income until the Second World War. Later, with the first significant expansion of the system in the 1960s (associated with the 1963 Robbins Report), student fees remained as part of the university funding structure but were paid on students' behalf by their home local education authority. Later still, with a far larger system, starting in 1998, tuition fees to be paid by students themselves were (re-)introduced and have been increased regularly since then, supported by a loan system. In England—the other nations of the UK have all taken somewhat different paths—tuition fees paid by students now, once again, account for the largest part of most universities' incomes, with fees in 2016/17 being £9,000 per year for UK and EU undergraduates—broadly similar to fees for in-state students at leading US public universities. Thus, in some nations, higher education shifts from being publicly provided at little or no cost to the student, to one where the taxpayer retreats from meeting the entire cost and with increased cost-sharing by the student/family as tuition fees are introduced and often then steadily increased.

Student tuition fees are everywhere a contentious issue. (Access to finance to cover living costs—equally significant for full-time students—is, illogically, usually less contentious.) On the one hand is the principled view that higher education is a right and access to it should be limited only by ability to benefit from it, not by an ability to pay. This is countered by supporters of tuition fees who argue that a government-backed loan system can deal with the 'ability to pay' argument; they would probably go on to argue that students will use their time at university more productively if they have a financial stake in a successful outcome. A more utilitarian objection to fees is that they may suppress student demand and that society will therefore not benefit from the highly trained people that would otherwise be produced. Supporters of fees can point out that, generally, demand has not been noticeably reduced where fees have been introduced; nor is there strong evidence that potential students from poorer backgrounds are deterred, assuming there is a carefully constructed loans scheme in place (the suggestion being that they might be more risk-averse than students from well-off families, even if loans were available). Finally, a practical objection to a fees-plus-loan system is that the costs of funding it upfront, and the difficulty of recovering loans from a mobile population over many years, makes the savings to the public finances so small as to be hardly worth the trouble.

The principled point put forward in favour of tuition fees is that the beneficiaries of higher education tend to be from better off than average backgrounds, and typically go on to achieve higher than average earnings over their lifetimes, often in relatively prestigious careers. Where is the equity, it is argued, in such individuals being subsidized from the taxes paid by lower income earners, often in jobs from which they derive little satisfaction?

The argument about student fees, then, is more than a technical one about finance: it goes to the heart of the university's relationship with its students, and to the university's relation with the state and society. In particular, do students paying significant levels of fees see themselves more as customers than as students in the traditional sense—and what does that mean for their relationship with their teachers? Does it mean that the university is just another organization providing a service to paying customers, rather than an institution with a unique role in civil society as a disinterested creator and disseminator of knowledge?

One area of university life that suggests that universities are not just another organization comes from their occasional roles as the focus of protest and even revolution, the radicals taking to the barricades usually being the students rather than the academics. The most famous incident is the 1968 student protests at the Sorbonne in Paris and at Berkeley, California, with rather more low-key events at the Universities of Essex, Warwick, and the LSE in Britain. Notoriously, students were shot and killed by security forces at Kent State University, Ohio, during protests over racial discrimination in 1970; and even more violent were the 1989 Tian'anmen Square protests in Beijing. More recently students have been heavily involved in Hong Kong's 'umbrella' demonstrations about democratic rights. Again in central Beijing, the May Fourth Movement of 1919 saw 3,000 students, mainly from Peking University (including a young Mao Zedong as one of its library assistants), demonstrating violently against foreign imperialism and the colonization of parts of China, as well as calling for new political solutions—all leading to the creation of the Chinese Communist Party in 1921. The common theme is, of course, young—and hence, understandably and appropriately, idealistic—people seeking to challenge what they see as outdated and discriminatory social mores, or unfair and corrupt political systems; and the common reaction of governments under such pressures is to close down university campuses for a period.

Less dramatically, the faculty in their academic research and publications often seek 'to speak truth to power' and thereby influence political change and social reform—occasionally ending up unemployed or worse during witch-hunts such as the anti-communist McCarthy era in 1950s America, or at times of religious turmoil such as the Reformation. Some would see the university as having a duty to be the conscience of society, and to use its autonomy and academic freedom to speak out against social and political injustices. Critics might dismiss the university as a location for left-wing academics to lead impressionable students astray, for fashionable fussing over political correctness within 'the therapeutic university' and on 'the medicalized campus', beset with demands about the need for 'safe spaces', 'speech codes', 'no platforming', 'bias response teams', and 'trigger warnings' or 'content warnings' lest emotionally vulnerable 'snowflake' students be confronted with challenging ideas or distressing facts. This last feature amounts, some assert, to the 'infantilization' of the university as higher education becomes merely the continuation of school and no longer an emancipatory experience: they fear the shutting down of the university's intellectual space and the constraining of the marketplace of ideas. And a final thought on 'the revolting student'—while in the past student protests and demonstrations seemed to be about seeking a better and fairer world, now they often focus more narrowly on who pays for universities, on the introduction of tuition fees, or on increases in fees. It seems probable that there will be increasing tension on the campus as the 'safe spaces' and 'trigger warnings' expectations of some students clash with the 'free speech' demands of others and also potentially with the university's commitment to 'academic freedom'.

A matter of judgement

All levels of education embody some form of assessment, and day-to-day life in universities, for students, teachers, and administrators, revolves to a large extent around its operation. Assessments include formal written examinations and coursework or assignments; universities use different mixes of these methods to determine the level of award made to students. Very little university-level assessment is of a right/wrong nature, other than where basic facts are involved—rather it consists of making judgements about (for instance) how evidence of various kinds has been selected and presented, and the extent to which ideas and theories have been understood, applied, and—importantly—challenged. Clearly, these are all matters on which reasonable people can disagree.

These considerations have, in many university systems, led to elaborate assessment processes, often involving two markers who do not know the student's identity ('blind marking') and sometimes where, additionally, one marker does not know who the other marker is ('double-blind marking'). The aim is to stop bias—conscious or unconscious—towards students who may be favoured for various reasons, as well as to try to ensure independent judgements by staff members. Not all university systems go to these lengths, however: in some European countries and elsewhere, the tradition of oral examinations, involving a single student and a single professor, continues, with all the scope for (at best) personal prejudice and (at worst) corruption that such a method invites; while in the US the academic delivery and also the grading of the course or module is usually by the same faculty member, often acting alone.

Students who feel that they have been treated unfairly have, in most countries, appeals processes open to them. In Britain and in most other countries, such appeals are, however, confined to procedural matters—not the academic judgement of the markers. This is the doctrine of judicial deference to the exercise of expert academic judgement, providing it has been properly exercised. It has been accepted by the British courts that to allow academic judgements to be challenged, providing that they have been made in conformity with the particular university's own regulations, would quickly lead to a situation in which every dissatisfied student would demand that their work be re-marked. This places a heavy responsibility on the academic staff who make up university examination boards: they are making essentially unchallengeable decisions which can have a profound effect on students' futures.

Quality and standards—what's the difference?

Everyone wants their university education to be of high quality—but what does this mean? Quality in higher education, in the sense of it being assessable and a matter for public and political consideration rather than gossip among university staff, is a relatively new idea, reflecting the expansion ('How do we know the expanded system is as good as we think the old one was?') and globalization ('How do we know that our system is as good as theirs?') of higher education. Many countries have an official (or, as in the US, a voluntary yet comprehensive) system of accreditation—either of whole institutions or of courses offered by them, or both. There are often legal restrictions on offering programmes that have not been accredited. This may offer a degree of consumer protection to students (most students only ever 'buy' one degree programme, so they are inexperienced and probably underinformed purchasers) and an assurance to public funding agencies that taxpayers' money is being well-spent. If the basis of accreditation is a judgement of how close a university is to the model provided by the nation's 'top' universities, then the system may also act as a means of asserting the (perhaps stifling) authority of these institutions and their professors.

But what is actually being measured in these accreditation processes? A key distinction is between standards and quality. Most people outside higher education expect universities to offer a high standard of education, and perhaps they assume that saying it is of high quality is another way of saying it is a high standard. But, strictly speaking, it is not. To borrow from the UK's Quality Assurance Agency (QAA) for higher education, *academic standards* are 'predetermined and explicit levels of achievement which must be reached for a student to be granted a qualification'. *Academic quality*, on the other hand, 'is a way of describing the effectiveness of everything that is done or provided by individual institutions, to ensure that the students have the best possible opportunity to meet the stated outcomes of their programmes and the academic standards of the awards they are seeking'. So quality is a process that could be broadly similar in all universities—and, in the UK, it is what (at present) the QAA inspects—whereas standards are benchmarks, which may, and do, differ between universities. It, therefore, follows (confusingly!) that a university may have high standards, yet fail a quality inspection; or apparently show the characteristics of high quality, yet have standards that are generally recognized (by professional bodies, say) as unacceptable. Furthermore, the standards to be achieved by students at a 'world-class' university, which demands high academic scores of its incoming students, will be different to those at a university serving a largely regional catchment, perhaps recruiting students with more modest examination results. It seems obvious that neither university would be helped by applying a common standard; though both should aspire to the same levels of quality in their teaching.

Moving on

So, the 'undergraduate' student completes the academic requirements of the degree course and duly becomes a 'graduate'; the degree being 'awarded' on passing all the examinations and then 'conferred' at a 'degree ceremony' (called 'commencement' in the US). And what next? Today, in countries with mass higher education systems, graduates go on to work in every economic sector, at just about every level. The idea of the 'graduate job', with the implication that organizations would recruit a handful of high-flying young people who would move inexorably to leadership positions, has to a large extent disappeared: for a long period now, a graduate job is a job that a graduate does. There are also concerns about graduate un- (or under-)employment. But many large organizations still invest considerable resources in recruiting what they consider to be the best graduates, from 'top' universities. There is a logic to this from the recruiter's point of view: these graduates have survived (it is assumed) a gruelling filtering process: progressing from school examinations to selection by the university through to the final award of a degree. The screening hypothesis, as it is often known, proposes that an important economic function of higher education is to identify talent in its various manifestations in this way, almost regardless of what might have been learned, so that employers are saved the trouble and uncertainty of talent-spotting themselves. This works even in countries where university standards are regarded as low by international measures: multinational companies will typically recruit from the 'best' local universities (however poor they may be comparatively), on the assumption that the brightest local young people (some of them at least, which is all that matters to an employer) will have found their way there.

Although the idea of graduate jobs may have faded, in most countries the prestigious professions—finance, law, the media, politics—are usually dominated by the graduates of the elite universities; sometimes, from just one university, usually in the capital city (England and the US are, because of different historical accidents, untypical in having elite universities elsewhere than in their capital city). This domination of professions by the elite universities is another factor that ensures that they stay elite: ambitious young people conclude that if they want to join these professional ranks, they too must strive to enter an elite university—which allows these universities to continue to select from among an exceptionally able pool of applicants. And, of course, the graduates of these universities, when in positions of influence, tend to make decisions which, perhaps unconsciously, favour the universities which they attended. In Britain, for example, Oxford and Cambridge Universities have a visibility in the media such that a normal reader or viewer would probably be surprised to learn that between them they educate only about 1.5 per cent of undergraduates in Britain. But, of course, their graduates are represented disproportionately in the media or in politics, and in other high-profile jobs or in money-making activities: a recent study asserts that Harvard leads globally in having the most millionaires among any university's graduates—in the UK, Cambridge, the LSE, and Oxford top the table; while other strong performers worldwide are INSEAD, Mumbai University, and the National University of Singapore.

In the rapidly evolving global economy, universities are called upon to meet needs that go far beyond those of the long established professions. Just as university research produced the electronic computer and most of the rest of the digital world, so today it is busy producing the currently unknown economy of tomorrow. This means that many of today's students will spend most of their working lives doing jobs that do not yet exist. Their teachers will hope that the intellectual ideas and approaches that they have passed on to their students will apply in future industrial revolutions as they have in past ones—that the key feature of *higher* education has been achieved in that the graduates have learned how to learn and how to think critically, as they reflectively and responsively adapt to changing ideas over the decades of their working lives. And a final comment on 'moving on' as graduates into society and the economy. Graduates from lower socio-economic groups who not only manage to get into higher education but also succeed in graduating (especially from an elite, high-brand university or college) may well see a welcome life-long payoff by way of career earnings for their personal investment in higher education, but they face a price in terms of social and family disruption; they are 'class migrants' moving from a working class background and taking up middle class careers and lifestyles.

Chapter 6
Working in universities and colleges: more than just a job?

In Chapter 1, we considered the idea and ideal of the university over the centuries since its creation in medieval Europe, and in Chapters 2 and 3 we looked at what the modern university does and what patterns we can detect in higher education delivery worldwide. In Chapter 4, we asked whether the university is a special organization, being exceptional in some way. In Chapter 5, we examined what it is like to be a student in the university, and in this chapter we think about working in one: whether, again, there is something exceptional about being an academic or whether, even if it once was, it is now just another job. As with the rest of this book, the many issues and themes flagged in this chapter can be followed up via the extensive Further Reading section.

But, first, what of employees other than the academics—the cleaners, lab technicians, librarians, clerical staff, catering staff, and many more—needed to keep the complex modern 'multiversity' functioning? Apart from the fact that the university on average offers reasonably congenial surroundings (especially those with the leafy campus format) and usually decent buildings, probably also fair human resource management procedures, there is nothing so very unusual for these groups to be working at a university rather than anywhere else (and the lack of car parking space will be the same wicked issue as everywhere!). They might have a greater sense of identity with and loyalty to a venerable old university and perhaps especially to a small cosy college. They may not feel so dedicated to a sprawling campus with over 50,000 students: it may then indeed be just like any other job or employer. That said, the proverbial departmental secretary or administrator is often a long-serving dedicated lynch-pin, much respected and valued by academics and generations of students alike; as also is, say, the wise college porter or the friendly cleaner, fondly remembered by cohorts of ex-students long after they have graduated (and forgotten their professors!).

Is it different for academics, for the faculty, for the professors? We have already noted that their primary sense of identity is often, and their dominant allegiance is usually, connected to their academic subject or discipline—to their guild or tribe—rather than to University X or Y where they currently happen to be placed. This is especially so for those whose research output will determine their reputation, employability, earnings, mobility, and promotion prospects. They will probably describe themselves as a physicist or philosopher, perhaps as a university academic, before they will label themselves as, say, a lecturer at Coketown University (although, doubtless, if their university is Oxford, Harvard, or some such elite institution, they will somehow get that mentioned). The ones at the research-focused institutions are unlikely to think of themselves as university 'teachers', not least because, unlike school teachers, they are not trained in or recruited for their teaching skills. Indeed, probably rarely does their academic department discuss pedagogy (despite the income or fees for teaching usually being a university's largest single source of funding, and often being used to subsidize the research mission)—although this is slowly changing in some countries, and even in their top universities, where the student becomes a fee-paying consumer.

So, the image was once of the very independent, even rather eccentric, and perhaps sometimes not very professional or productive academic as a figure of some standing in the university as an organization and indeed in the wider community (academics have never, however, got themselves together as a powerful professional group like the doctors or the lawyers, and have never had a truly influential professional body like those of, say, nurses or architects). And this 'once' was when universities were far fewer, when only some 10–15 per cent of young people went into higher education. The sub-genre of fiction known as 'the campus novel' plots the trajectory of falling status for most academics, as the decline of donnish dominion tracks the 'massification' of higher education when now there are three times as many universities and students—more universities, more students, more faculty means none is any longer deemed so special, so exceptional. The pompous professor boss of *Lucky Jim* (Amis, 1954) thus becomes the 1960s, manipulative, lefty lecturer, Howard Kirk, in *The History Man* (Bradbury, 1975); and then is the feeble and sad victim of manipulation by self-aggrandizing management in the university fiction of recent decades (Figure 8).

8. University of East Anglia (1961–6; by Denys Lasdun)—a fine example of the expansionist 1960s university campus architecture, here externally plate glass, but brick at Sussex, and tiled blocks at Warwick.

The wider literature on universities bemoans the commercialization and commodification of academe, and laments the change from the happy days when universities, supposedly, just were meant 'to be' themselves and were not expected 'to be for' in terms of contributing to the economy (Box 9).

Box 9. On university power politics, 1970s style

Compared to the university politics of the 1930s (Box 6) or of the 1900s (Box 7), Malcolm Bradbury in *The History Man* (1975) portrays the manipulative and scheming Dr Howard Kirk as 'the trendiest of radical tutors at a fashionable campus university' in 1972; here a sociology department meeting gets (slowly and fractiously) underway:

Then the alarm clock of Benita Pream, the administrative assistant, pings; Professor Marvin coughs very loudly and waves his arms. He looks up and down the long table, and says: 'Can we now come to order, gentlemen?' Immediately the silence breaks; many arms go up, all around the table; there is a jabber of voices. 'May I point out, Mr Chairperson, that of the persons in this room you are addressing as "gentlemen", seven are women?' says Melissa Todoroff... 'Doesn't the phrase itself suggest we are somehow normally in a state of disorder?' asks Roger Fundy. 'Can I ask whether under Standing Orders of Senate we are bound to terminate this meeting in three and a half hours? And, if so whether the Chairman thinks an agenda of thirty-four items can be seriously discussed under those limitations, especially since my colleagues will presumably want to take tea?'... 'May I ask if it is the wish of this meeting that we should have a window open?'.... The pile-drivers thump outside; the arguments within continue.... Benita Pream's alarm has pinged at 14.00 hours, according to her own notes; it is 14.20 before the meeting has decided how long it is to continue, and whether it is quorate, and if it should have the window open, and 14.30 before Professor Marvin has managed to sign the minutes of the last meeting...[Item 1—'An uncontentious item, I think' says the Chairman—takes an hour up to tea-time, and the nadir is reached when a] recommendation that Senate be asked to nominate the members of the select committee who will nominate the members of the working party who will make proposals for nominations so that the departmental meeting can nominate the external examiners is defeated, on the grounds that this would be an external interference from Senate in the affairs of the department: even though, as the chair points out, the department cannot in any case nominate external examiners, but only recommend names to Senate, who will nominate them.

If the academics were playing pettily pathetic power politics at their departmental meetings in the late 1960s and early 1970s, their students were more busily and energetically revolting—protests and occupations at the Sorbonne, at Berkeley, at Columbia, at Cornell, and (rather more low-key) at Harvard, Yale, and Princeton. The UK 'action' was even more muted, but still disturbing for bewildered university leaders—at the LSE, at Essex, at Warwick, at Cambridge, and at Oxford. In a 1969 post-mortem on these troubled times at Oxford the puzzled dons talked of 'the exaggerations, naïve expectations, and concealed fallacies in the amalgam of student revolutionary ideas' and of 'scatter-brained and muddle-headed' Oxford participants in the recent protests, demonstrations, and occupations seeking 'political, economic, and social revolution' in a context of universities appearing 'both to sustain the structure of a corrupt society and to reflect it'; the student idealists sought 'a democratic university', with echoes of the medieval student-centred university model at Bologna discussed in Chapter 1 and in Box 2. Fifty years on, those revolting students are now retiring from thoroughly middle class and non-revolutionary careers as lawyers, media pundits, and similar.

Once the university was run by the professors for the professors, as the idealized and perfect form from the perspective of professors; and this 'once' being when it was (briefly, in the 1960s) generously funded by the state as a free publicly provided good, before government largesse began to be curtailed, and economies had to be suffered along with demands for accountability, and (in some countries) efforts (again, as in earlier times) had to be made to recruit fee-paying student customers. Back then it was fashionable to talk of 'collegiality' in decision-making, even of the university as organizationally 'loosely coupled', if not indeed an 'organized anarchy'. Managing academics was likened to herding cats or getting butterflies to fly in formation. But along came 1990s corporatism and managerialism as (supposedly) a 'neoliberal' agenda: administration bloomed and the faculty lost their power and influence in most universities (although much less so among the research elite). So now many academics may feel as managed, within a formal hierarchy, as any other employee in many other workplaces; and they may also feel that their managers are less competent and less well-trained than managers in other organizations—a complaint they have in common with other professionals or experts who have somehow to be managed in such settings as schools and hospitals.

While in some nations the professor is still a figure to be respected if not revered, the question does arise in the US and UK of whether the faculty brought upon themselves their decline of status. Were they too readily involved in political protest in the 1960s, many joining their (back then not much younger) students at the barricades? Were they rumbled for operating a 'ProfScam' by being poor teachers, lazy researchers, waffly writers of trendy jargon-filled trivia that was passed off as academic output; squabbling among their various sub-tribes about obscure issues and neglecting their students? Or did they just suffer in the general passing of a deferential age and its being replaced by a cynicism about professionals of all kinds and a reaction to one-time deference within explicit social hierarchies? Probably for all these reasons the professors as a whole have lost status and in many cases, comparatively, pay and perks—but some can still carve out enviable lifestyles in comfortable environments, enjoying their very special benefits of academic tenure and academic freedom (as well as in some countries still enjoying high social status).

These two legal concepts of tenure and of academic freedom as unique to universities in many but certainly not all countries need to be explained. The academic, it is claimed, must be able to undertake research on and teach about areas that may upset some vested interests (including established conventions of thinking in academe itself where they are threatening the prevailing paradigms of fixed interpretation and set explanations). To be protected from dismissal for treading on toes, he or she needs 'academic freedom' and that is best ensured by having 'tenure' whereby there can't be dismissal other than for 'good cause'—not simply for saying or writing what others find inconvenient or annoying. Moreover, the university itself is often said in some countries to benefit from its academic freedom in the form of 'institutional autonomy'—politicians being unable simply to shut down the campus when students or faculty annoy them. However, just how legally solid and valid are these concepts, and are they abused by faculty?

The strength of the meaning of academic freedom varies hugely across nations, being enshrined in the constitution or embedded into its higher education law in some European countries, and being merely a few words rather randomly fitted into an Act to do with funding universities in the UK. In the US, academic freedom depends on court cases, and more recently these have tended to narrow down the scope of this freedom. A professor may mistakenly believe he or she is free to, as it were, sound off on anything and everything; but, in fact, he or she is only academically free to take a stance within the area of his or her academic expertise, keeping carefully within the bounds of normal academic discourse. And certainly, this academic freedom does not in any way protect against the law of the land in terms of, say, racism, discrimination, national security, or defamation. Nor is the academic necessarily free to criticize publicly the management of his or her own university (aside perhaps from the protection that any whistle-blowing employee is meant to receive). In the end, indeed, academic freedom is only as secure as the rule of law and the independence of the judiciary within the constitution of a given nation—which is to say that, in more countries than one might fear, the university is potentially only a couple of steps away from being forced to submit to the demands of a domineering political group sweeping to power and sweeping away constitutional niceties (Box 10).

Box 10. On academic freedom

There is much said and written but little really understood about the concept of academic freedom, and here are some statements or protections within different legal jurisdictions.

In Austrian law:

> the termination or dismissal of a member of the scientific and artistic [humanities?] university staff shall be null and void if an official notification has been issued as a result of an opinion or method advocated by such staff member in the course of his/her research, artistic or teaching activities.

In EU law the EU Charter of Fundamental Rights of the European Union (Article 13) declares:

> the arts and scientific research shall be free of constraint [and] academic freedom shall be respected.

In French law:

> researchers and teachers are fully independent and enjoy full freedom of speech in the course of their research and teaching activities, providing they respect principles of tolerance and objectivity.

In German law:

> art and science research and teaching are free [but] freedom
> of teaching does not absolve from loyalty to the constitution.

In English law:

> academic staff have freedom within the law to question
> and test received wisdom, and to put forward new ideas
> and controversial or unpopular opinions, without placing
> themselves in jeopardy of losing their jobs or privileges
> they may have at their institutions.

The UK Higher Education and Research Act 2017, at the time of
passing though the Lords, was amended to provide for legislative
protection of institutional academic freedom by this wording:

> universities are autonomous institutions and must uphold
> the principles of academic freedom and speech . . . [and
> also] must ensure that they promote freedom of thought
> and expression, and freedom from discrimination [as well
> as being] free to act as critics of government and the
> conscience of society.

As eventually enacted, however, it simply stresses that the newly
created Office for Students as the new regulator of universities
'must have regard to the need to protect the institutional
autonomy of English higher education providers'. This idea of
'institutional autonomy' is later defined as the 'freedom' to
'determine' what to teach, how to teach it, who should teach,
and whom to teach—as well as invoking the academic freedom
of individual faculty as noted above in the wording from the 1988
legislation. It is very clear, therefore, that English universities are
not in any way public bodies as emanations of the state; are not
controlled by government; and can continue as more independent
and autonomous entities than most universities around the world.

(*continued*)

Box 10. Continued

In the 1997 UNESCO Statement:

> [faculty possess] the right without constriction by prescribed doctrine, to freedom of teaching and discussion, freedom in carrying out research and disseminating and publishing the results thereof, freedom to express freely their opinion about the institution or system in which they work, freedom from institutional censorship.

In American law (from the 1957 US Supreme Court *Sweezy* case):

> The essentiality of freedom in the community of American universities is almost self-evident. No one should underestimate the vital role in a democracy that is played by those who guide and train our youth. To impose any strait jacket upon intellectual leaders in our colleges and universities would imperil the future of our Nation.... Teachers and students must always remain free to inquire, to study and to evaluate, to gain new maturity and understanding; otherwise our civilisation will stagnate and die.... It is the business of a university to provide that atmosphere which is most conducive to speculation, experiment and creation. It is an atmosphere in which there prevail 'the four essential freedoms' of a university to determine for itself on academic grounds who may teach, what may be taught, how it should be taught, and who may be admitted to study.

And from *Keyishian* (USSC, 1967):

> The classroom is peculiarly the 'marketplace of ideas'. The Nation's future depends upon leaders trained through wide exposure to that robust exchange of ideas which discovers truth.

In the 1940 'Statement of Principles on Academic Freedom' issued by the AAUP (American Association of University Professors):

Teachers are entitled to full freedom in research and in the publication of results.... Teachers are entitled to freedom in the classroom in discussing their subject but should be careful not to introduce into their teaching controversial matter which has no relation to their subject.

And the earlier 1915 version referred to freedom of inquiry and research; freedom of teaching within the university or college; and freedom of extramural utterance and action.

In the US context, tenure is an employment practice for some (albeit increasingly fewer) faculty that is usually linked to the concept of academic freedom, but it is clearly possible to have the latter without the former—tenure was abolished, for instance, in the UK by legislation in 1988, but with no detrimental effect upon the academic freedom of faculty; and indeed recently in some US states their governments have also abolished tenure across the public university system (notably within the University of Wisconsin).

The concept of academic freedom is controversial, being more narrowly interpreted by some as simply a protection from external interference for the academic guild going about its professional task of seeking and disseminating truth in a scholarly way. Others promote it in grand (even grandiose) terms as a licence for academics to critique anything and everything as 'the conscience of society' with a duty 'to speak truth to power'. The former version is the one recognized in American law; interestingly, something closer to the latter at one point in the legislative process looked like being enshrined for the UK in the 2017 legislation on universities, but in the end (as noted earlier) it was not enacted. In essence, the further the individual academic strays from his or her subject expertise and/or begins to express opinions in an unscholarly and politically partisan fashion, the less the protective device of academic freedom can be invoked.

(*continued*)

Box 10. Continued

The academic is then left relying on the general free speech rights of any citizen. Indeed, the academic freedom of faculty may in some countries be no greater than, no more special than, the free speech rights of any citizen.

Moreover, the concept of academic freedom, where it is even acknowledged in law, is often attached to the institution rather than to the academic. The latter's personal academic freedom, therefore, is still constrained by being an employee of the university in terms, for instance, of having to teach the approved course syllabus for, say, alchemy. Failure to do so would be insubordination (although a suitably scholarly article criticizing the teaching of alchemy in universities as now being out of date and lacking scientific credibility would probably be protected by the writer invoking academic freedom—ditto astrology or homeopathy). In short, the idea of academic freedom does not extend as widely as many faculty assume and does not make them as exceptional or privileged as most would like. This can be especially the case if an academic were to assume that this freedom would give him or her solid cover for aggressive criticism of the university's governance and management. Nor does the law accept that every professor on campus—under some assumption that academic freedom justifies widespread collegiality or shared governance in decision-making—has a veto or even a vote on, say, increases in the price of coffee in the refectory or the charge for car parking.

Academic tenure is unknown in some university systems and, while it did exist in the UK, it was abolished by legislation in the 1980s. Where it does not apply as a legal concept the normal employment protection legislation governs the academic–university contract of employment, with academics in some countries being state employees (i.e. civil servants). In the US, where general employment protection laws are much weaker than in the UK, other EU countries, Canada, Australia, and New Zealand, the award of tenure was and is greatly prized, since employers have wide discretion to dismiss normal employees. Nonetheless, again, their status still depends on court cases interpreting the meaning of academic tenure. Although US universities are still reluctant to embark on the cumbersome process of dismissing tenured professors, the trend in recent cases is in the institution's favour where the subject area is unable to recruit students (redundancy) or where the individual is misbehaving (being 'uncollegial') in ways that have nothing to do with the proper exercise of his or her legitimate academic freedom. Moreover, in the US only an increasingly small percentage of faculty enjoy tenure, since there, as in the UK, universities are getting more of their undergraduate teaching delivered cheaply by low-paid, casual/adjunct labour employed by the course or by graduate students rather than by traditional, full-time, permanent and tenured academics.

There is an extensive and expanding polemical literature asserting that the professor, especially in the US, is pampered inside the expensively padded faculty lounge; overprotected by undeserved and unnecessary tenure which distorts the academic labour market; and is abusing academic freedom to pontificate widely and wildly. He or she is allegedly neglecting what should be the core and key activity of undergraduate teaching, while fussing about publishing vast amounts of unread and unreadable papers in obscure academic journals where these academics self-reference and mutually cite each other; allegedly content for underpaid and overworked adjunct lecturers on casual employment contracts to do all the heavy lifting as an exploited academic underclass fed by the cynical overproduction of PhD students misled into thinking an academic career awaits them. Supposedly, the professor is hiding behind the battle cry of academic freedom to avoid professional accountability, and is fixated with issues of political correctness. The charge-sheet is lengthy and growing!—although actual evidence for the prosecution is not always convincing. And, these stern critics declare, the idea of academic freedom is all the more irrelevant in the context of modern mass higher education when the bulk of teaching is now for skills and competencies vocational degrees that can hardly be said to touch upon the search for ultimate truths and to impinge upon delicate areas which might upset those in power. The same applies to the concept of tenure—if university academics are just glorified school teachers, albeit at tertiary level, they can be treated as normal employees.

We assess in Chapter 7 whether radical, transformational, disruptive change will occur in higher education or whether the university of 2050 will be broadly similar to that of 1950 and 2000; whether the specialness and exceptionalism for academics of working in the university will remain if they can indeed be fairly said at present to be as cosseted as their critics assert. In fact, some detect such change already—talking of the fall of the faculty and the rise of what they criticize as overpaid and undertalented administrators spouting managerial psycho-babble (critics perceive and condemn the spread of 'administrative blight' across the campus and the curse of 'administrative bloat'). The professor has been marginalized, donnish dominion is finished, tenure is only for the declining few as a licence to pursue research interests for the greater good. Being an academic is no longer special for the professor, with the university no longer being an exceptional place to work. That said, to those working under rigid regimes in, say, factories, shops, or call centres, the relative freedom of the professor's working day, and especially his or her long breaks between teaching terms (roughly 15/20 weeks of one and 30/35 of the other), will seem rather attractive, no matter how indignantly the professor protests about long hours in term-time; about spending vacation time on research; or about needing one sabbatical term off in seven to update lecture notes.

In considering the working life of academics in the modern university as part of massified higher education, a further word is needed on their tribes and territories, and on their sense of professional identity. Perhaps the old idea of academic subjects or disciplines is now giving way to interdisciplinarity as the guiding concept for, or driver of, academic organization and working life? Or maybe the professors are now just managed professionals, their academic autonomy and power vastly reduced? Are the organizational structures of the university changing, along with the processes of teaching and learning, and academic identities? And are all these aspects of the university, of its organizational culture, impacted by the commercialization and marketization of higher education, and not only in the Anglo-Saxon nations but across Europe and in Asia? Yet, amid all that change (that may well induce 'change fatigue' for the many university and college staff) is the traditional, subject-based, academic department still the core organizational unit with which the average member of faculty most identifies?—and which remains relatively unchanged in its structure and culture? The answers are probably, 'Yes', to all those questions: the university is changing and adapting as it has for centuries, just as (in terms of UK university fiction) the 1950s university of professorial hierarchy and rigid academic subjects portrayed in Amis's *Lucky Jim* (Box 11) became the fizzing political turmoil and cross-disciplinary, trendy 'schools' of the (1970s) *The History Man* (Bradbury) and then morphed into the 1980s entrepreneurial university of *A Very Peculiar Practice* (Davies). Similarly, the changing organizational culture in healthcare: the dynamics of the hospital hierarchy and professional interactions in the recent US TV series *House* are very different from the era of the all-powerful matron and consultant in the 1960s UK *Carry On, Doctor* films—or even the US 1960s *Dr Kildare*.

One major change over the past decade or so has certainly been a diversification and blurring of professional identities in universities, and hence the rise of 'blended' roles where academics and specialized administrators merge so as better to deliver higher education in the age of massification; demands for accountability for the use of public funds just as taxpayer austerity reduces

Box 11. On the stuffiness and amateurism of the 1950s university

In Kingsley Amis's *Lucky Jim* (1954), we get a vivid picture of the stifling hierarchy of the 1950s sleepy English provincial university, a cloying culture that was challenged and shaken up by the student (and staff) rebels of the 1960s (Box 9):

> Welch was talking yet again about his concert. How had he become Professor of History, even at a place like this? By published work? No. By extra good teaching? No in italics. Then how? As usual, [Jim] Dixon shelved this question, telling himself that what mattered was that this man had decisive power over his future, at any rate until the next four or five weeks were up. Until then he must try to make Welch like him, and one way of doing that was, he supposed, to be present and conscious while Welch talked about concerts. But did Welch notice who else was there while he talked, and, if he noticed did he remember, and if he remembered would it affect such thoughts as he had already?

Amis may have had in mind Bruce Truscot's *Red Brick University* and its critique of the amateurism of university academics—on the life of a professor, he commented:

> The life of a well-established, middle-aged professor in the Arts faculty of a modern [1940s] university can, if he likes to make it so, be one of the softest jobs to be found on the earth's surface.... The professor, enjoying a tenure so secure that, until the date of his retirement arrives, it is almost impossible for him to be ejected except for some grave delinquency....

And on the lecture system, he notes that the lecturer will not have had 'any training whatsoever' in teaching because 'universities are amateurish bodies' with the results of their 'laxity' being 'appalling' by way of poor teaching—whether there should be mandatory teacher training for academics is still being debated some eighty years later! Truscot was a pseudonym to keep secret the real identity of this whistle-blower; he was, in fact, a professor of Spanish at the University of Liverpool.

Similarly, from Michael Innes in his *Death at the President's Lodgings* (1936)—one of the earliest examples of the Oxford college murders genre—we hear:

> It is in our universities that the conservative spirit finds its most perfect expression. Long after the reform of our ecclesiastical institutions, medieval habits survive within these venerable establishments.

Innes was the crime-writing pseudonym of J.I.M. Stewart, who lectured at Leeds University and then at Queen's Belfast in the 1930s and 1940s before becoming an Oxford don—under his real name, he published in the 1970s a quintet of novels about college life, *A Staircase in Surrey*, to match Snow's novels about Cambridge—see Box 6. In these novels Stewart give us glimpses of a time when, as discussed in Box 8, admission to Oxford (as also to elite US universities and colleges) was shaped by the idea that suitable young men of sound character were to be prepared as leaders, and that selection purely on academic merit would risk filling the college with clever but dull chaps. It was seen as desirable that

> a body of undergraduates ought to be a mixed lot; that some should read [study] and some should row.... [Thus a college] had a particular responsibility to educate, if remotely educable, those boys whose inherited wealth or tradition [upbringing] was particularly likely to promote to positions of public responsibility later on.... We'd take on boys we liked and begin with the alphabet if they needed it.... [But by the 1970s] the pitifully thick, the incorrigibly

(continued)

Box 11. Continued

idle, even the pronouncedly inane: these, however socially
acceptable, were now, except through error or chicanery,
ruled out [for admission].

(And so there was room by 1972 for Palfreyman, distinctly
lacking, as a Mancunian grammar school tyke, either 'wealth or
tradition'!) Indeed, even women were being admitted to the
hitherto male-only Oxbridge colleges by 1979, having stormed
Harvard, Yale, and Princeton just a few years earlier.

such funds; tuition fees driving student consumerism; increased
competition among institutions; entrepreneurial activities
supporting the knowledge economy and regional development;
and efforts to engender civic engagement. Thus, there are more
part-time posts, more fixed-term contracts, more signs of labour
mobility nationally and internationally, more new job titles (the
medieval 'registrar' title becomes a 'chief operating officer' or
'COO'!); more and different promotion criteria; more training
and career-development opportunities; more career pathways.
And perhaps amid all this adaptation the university of 2050
becomes a more varied and interesting, albeit also a more
demanding and exhausting, place of work than that of 1950,
1970, or even 1985? Or perhaps it still amounts to a dispiriting
decline for the professors in terms of self-regulation and
autonomy, professional and social status, work satisfaction?
On balance, however, it is hard to deny that the academic
profession is being degraded in the context of the mass-managed,
corporatist, modern form of the university—measured in terms
of the decline in such key features of academic life over recent
decades as autonomy, flexibility, respect and status, collegiality,
and even commensality (staff clubs, senior common rooms,
departmental tea bars are all being phased out in the name of
economy and efficiency).

There remains, however, one very special, exceptional, and pretty well unique feature of being a professor—the concept of judicial deference in every legal jurisdiction to the proper exercise of academic judgement. Providing the faculty teach the specified quantity of material the university recruitment marketing has stipulated or promised for the degree course and also examine the students in accordance with any stated procedures, the courts will not attempt to second-guess student claims based on the issue of alleged poor teaching quality. The academic in many legal systems is, apart from judges themselves, the last professional group to benefit from this legal immunity against challenge on the basis of incompetence. There may be internal student complaints procedures and external quality audit regimes, but there, as in the courts, the issue of academic judgement in terms of what is taught and how it is taught is beyond challenge, unlike for doctors, engineers, architects, and other such professionals who can be found to have been professionally negligent, to have failed to meet the standard of the reasonably competent doctor, engineer, etc., by the courts or by their professional bodies. There is no such idea of academic malpractice, of professorial negligence.

Why? Because it is a matter of public policy and judicial common sense. When higher education was a free publicly provided good and when only 5–10 per cent of young people enjoyed access to it, in policy terms it seemed unnecessary for such privileged students to be allowed to complain about it; and anyway no court would want to spend valuable time trying to decide on the basis of expert witnesses whether the lectures in quantum mechanics or on Kant were of appropriate quality; whether the essay concerned should have been graded A rather than B; or whether the exam mark should have been 65 per cent rather than 56 per cent. Thus, in the common law countries the student customer is unable to sue the university in the private law of contract for supposed poor quality of teaching delivered under a student–university contract to educate; or under the law of negligence, in the private law of tort. In the civil code nations the arena for the righting of student grievances is usually some sort of administrative tribunal operating under public law, but here too student complaints based on alleged poor teaching will not be entertained. Academics do not have a true professional body as do doctors, dentists, engineers, and almost all other such professional groups that can strike the negligent academic off its register, taking away his or her licence to practise. The faculty have never wanted to organize themselves in this self-regulating way, still less have they wanted to scrutinize each other's professional standards.

But, as in steadily more countries higher education is ceasing to be a free public service and tuition fees are being introduced and then progressively hiked, it is no longer the preserve of the privileged few and it is no longer the case that becoming a graduate almost guarantees employment in a suitable well-paid career as it might have done a generation ago. The question has to be, therefore, when, rather than if, this privilege of legal immunity for academics and academe is likely to be abolished as being anachronistic, either by a decision of a nation's supreme court or by legislation with politicians seeing the fee-paying student customer as being in need of greater consumer protection. Moreover, when the nature of the degree courses being taught in the age of mass higher or indeed tertiary education is more a matter of skills and competencies vocational credentials, and where there can be some certainty and consistency about appropriate curriculum content and efficient teaching methods—rather than the teaching of, say, fuzzy philosophy or cutting-edge physics—the role of the court in assessing students' claims or of some other adjudicator/ombudsman for aggrieved students becomes simpler. It becomes clearer whether there has been a failure to deliver the quality of teaching that a reasonably competent academic and university should and could manage. Government policy in an increasing number of nations towards reshaping the university by including much needed regulation of the competitive, fees-based higher education market has shifted higher education from being a public good to being a private good. This question of special academic immunity against failing to provide teaching of appropriate quality will eventually have to be addressed—probably via its removal. The result may well be that being an academic becomes a rather less exceptional profession and that teaching in a university becomes rather more just another place to work.

Finally—is the university a happy place, in which either to work or be a student? The number of students seeking counselling has certainly increased greatly in recent years in many nations. But that does not automatically mean that being at university has caused them stress as opposed to it feeling like a safe space and time to get help for long-standing problems. Certainly, however, the mass-produced student of the 2010s has understandably far more concerns about future employment prospects than the authors' 1970s generation of far fewer graduates (and, in the US, Australia, and England, they will be graduating with growing levels of debt compared to the free ride enjoyed by students in the 1960s and 1970s). Surveys of faculty routinely reveal declining morale in many universities (especially among the older academics), with this unhappiness usually being directed at the seemingly impersonal and domineering 'management', at the unthinking use of performance indicators, at the university being devalued in its role as the conscience and critic of society. In some countries the university will be a focal point for bitter political and deep social tensions, often representing a new and better future for youth—and being resented for that by older conservative generations.

Can morale be managed; can faculty be managed; can the university be managed? The university has over centuries proved to be capable of re-inventing itself while also broadly retaining its core shape: teaching within the academic subject or discipline relying on its key employees (the faculty); and being self-managed (perhaps sometimes doing so just too loosely or collegially). Probably astute institutional leadership can indeed add value and 'manage' success without seeming to do so if it can engender across the campus a sense of purposeful engagement in an academic community. Ideally this community should have clear and widely accepted values; function in a professional, transparent, and honest way; learn from and absorb good practice from elsewhere; and use corporate self-knowledge to be reflective, responsive, and adaptable while retaining a strong sense of the core mission and also of its key values—to preserve for, and disseminate to, future generations our societies' cumulative learning through its high-quality teaching. As such an entity, it should also add to the stock of this accumulated learning along the way through its research activity. The university able to do all that will be indeed not only a successful university but also a special place and even perhaps a happy place in which to work, of which to be a member.

Chapter 7
Futures for the university and college

What are the mission and shape, the structure and culture, the purposes and ambitions of the university in the coming decades? What is it to 'be' a university now and what is the university now seen 'to be for'? What might change by 2050? Is it a matter of steady evolution, careful adaptation, gentle reinvention?—or a future of instability and disruptive innovation, of radical change, of absolute transformation? And, come what may, by way of radical change, perhaps with a few elite universities as oases of calm, still operating within a protected sphere? Is the future an opportunity for, or a threat to, the university? Does the University of the Future look more like the University of the Past than the University of the Present, or is it to be an entirely different idea and place from that which we have ever seen or now experience? Will the university continue to be, as some have seen it, that most versatile of institutions?—Clark Kerr once noting that, of the eighty-five entities in the Western world created by 1520 and which still existed over 450 years later, seventy were universities. Kerr commented that these universities were managing to appear to outsiders to be the least changed of all institutions, yet their insiders knew very well that they had changed hugely and would continue to do so. Whatever we write here by way of predicting the future of (or indeed a possible range of futures for) the university will (almost) certainly be wrong—that is about the only certainty in the art of prediction.

From the point of view of policy-makers, the functions of universities began to be seen in a different light once the ideas behind human capital theory, associated with the work of the economists Gary Becker and Robert Barro, began to gain currency from the 1960s as another strand to the claimed public benefit created by higher education. Spending money (whether public or private) on education came to be seen as a national investment rather than a cost. Just as a factory might invest in new machinery in order to improve productivity, and therefore profits, so, the theory suggested, a state should invest in education to increase its stock of skilled workers in order to enhance national wealth. In an increasingly competitive world, investment in higher education to produce more people with advanced skills—rather than the basic skills, which every country could have—began to seem, for rich countries, not merely desirable, but essential.

Human capital theory continues for many commentators to underlie one way of looking at what universities do now, and may do in the future. Although the ways in which economies will work in future decades is unknowable, higher education will continue to have a vital role in producing the high-quality human capital which these economies will need. This means somehow young people must be educated to do jobs that do not yet exist, in industries still to be created. A young person entering university around 2020 will probably be at the peak of his or her career in around 2050: even at the current rate of social and technological change, he or she will certainly inhabit a different world.

The formation of human capital, however, could be achieved by means other than the universities we have come to know over recent centuries—in principle, anyway, although it seems not to have happened significantly in practice so far. But human capital theory explains only part of what universities do. As we noticed, higher education performs a sifting or selection process for employers and others, sparing them the tedium and cost of selecting from the population at large and permitting them to look only at the smaller proportion who have successfully negotiated the hurdles set by higher education. But there is more to it: graduating from certain universities acts as a signalling process, showing that you are part of an elite group of graduates. As we have noted, this supports the perpetuation of national elites, and, we may confidently assume, the universities from which they came. Different, but still important, signals are sent as a result of being a graduate of other classes of institution, with reputations that may change over time (albeit rather slowly). It is hard to imagine how this complex, subtle signalling process could be replicated by some non-institutional, bureaucratic, educational structure.

These two considerations—human capital formation, and the sifting and signalling processes—both hard to replicate without a national higher education structure, suggest to us that universities have a relatively assured future. But such a future based on the instrumental view of the contribution made by universities will, we assert, also continue to rest on the concept of liberal education. It is this combination that puts the 'higher' into higher education, and differentiates the university from other forms of tertiary education. That said, we can detect a possible swing from the government belief over recent decades in the idea of ever-expanding higher education to a new stress on vocational education and training (VET) as a more direct preparation for employment (including via a growth of apprenticeships linked to post-secondary education not delivered in universities), and with taxpayer subsidy shifting accordingly at the expense of universities. The trick for universities might be to find ways to add in an academic dimension to this training-on-the-job, vocational route focused on the (hitherto often underfunded) further education or community college system.

The landscape of change

We have already noted the historical role of universities in providing the advanced skills needed by their societies. This will continue, with

9. **Central Hall, University of York (1968; by Robert Matthew, Johnson-Marshall, and Partners)—a striking feature of the 1960s campus. Such a 'great hall' is commonly used by universities for degree ceremonies (or 'commencement', in US terminology). The 1900s great hall at the University of Birmingham and the slightly later one in the Wills Building at the University of Bristol are especially 'grand' examples.**

a focus on the contribution of the university to the knowledge economy and its role in building the knowledge society—and still conferring degrees (Figure 9). Perhaps a new model will emerge for this new century, involving a research-centred, flagship, 'hub' university with associated clusters of campuses, different from the multiversity model that has dominated the second half of the 20th century. And some predict the emergence of super-hubs or global knowledge hubs in the US (say, San Francisco with Los Angeles, plus Boston, and also New York); in Europe (probably London and Munich); and in Asia (possibly Beijing, Shanghai, Hong Kong, and Singapore). Others anticipate the development of major players operating globally, on a massive scale, via a vast digital-learning operation but perhaps also with a network of 'micro-campuses' in partnership with selected local universities.

So, we can at least list a range of drivers of likely change, even if we are not able to predict exactly what direction they will push the university of 2020 by, say, 2050. Universities will take part in increasing cross-border and inter-institutional collaboration, as a network of partnerships in a globalized higher education world—although the World Trade Organization has had only limited success in introducing free trade in fields such as higher education, legal services, and healthcare—at least when compared with the extent of globalization over recent decades that has resulted in the generally low-tariff movement of physical goods.

An associated concern is the financial vulnerability of some universities, and indeed of entire higher education systems, if the global flow of lucrative high-fees international students is interrupted by geopolitical shocks—and especially where there has been massive borrowing to fund campus renewal and development. The recent signs of a reaction against globalization generally, including the international movement of students, would spell financial disaster for some US, UK, and Australian universities.

New digital learning modes may become more effective—although this promise seems much-heralded and long-delayed—so allowing an increase in remote learning as well as supporting on-campus teaching and learning.

But the build-up of un-/under-employed graduates within many nations that have expanded (or over-expanded) higher education in recent decades may create a backlash, with young people questioning the economic value of going to university, especially if they have incurred significant costs in going there. The erosion of the graduate-earnings premium relative to the growth of graduate debt will accentuate these concerns. Those governments that have introduced tuition fees may need to review their level relative to public subsidy of undergraduate higher education, the interest rates applied to graduate-loans debt, and the intergenerational fairness of such loans schemes.

At the same time, higher education has not been, and will not be, just about individuals 'learning stuff': the institutional framework is vital. So there may be enhanced segmentation and fragmentation, with even greater attention being given to institutional hierarchies, as universities seek their particular niche in a more diversified higher education marketplace.

This may lead to a blurring of boundaries between the traditional public university and private newcomers, and even between the charitable not-for-profits and commercial for-profit universities and colleges.

But segmentation may be countered by the tendency of universities towards *isomorphism* (i.e. all seeking to be like each other) and *filiopietism* (i.e. all seeking to be like venerable institutions such as Harvard or Oxford).

A broader issue is whether higher education growth has now peaked in many rich countries—although there may be opportunities for universities to offer courses for the increasing proportion of the population entering the 'Third Age', either as recreation or as re-skilling for re-entry to work at least on a part-time basis.

Given this range of change factors, all of which may be observed today to a greater or lesser extent around the world, it becomes extremely difficult to predict the future shape of higher education—any of these factors might increase at a rate that pushes particular higher education systems into new modes of operating. This might involve creating new shapes within a landscape incorporating elite, mass, niche, local, life-long, and vocational learning institutions; or universities might be operating as purely public or private, or as (semi-) privatized public entities, within a fully open market or a quasi-market. As an instance of the potential pace and extent of change, no informed observer ten years ago would have predicted that English universities at the bottom of most league tables would be charging undergraduate tuition fees of £9,000-plus a year alongside institutions such as Oxford, Cambridge, and UCL—with important consequences in many areas of student and institutional life (such as students needing part-time, term-time, paid work and the rise of the student consumer). There is also the fact that recent graduates from English universities appear now, as a result of £9,000 pa tuition fees and the rent costs for the high proportion living away from the parental home while attending 'uni', to be the most indebted worldwide (owing some £50,000 each, added to which is compound interest at 3 per cent above inflation—a total amount about a third of which some predict will never be fully paid off during the thirty years' loan period at *c*.10 per cent of annual income above some £20,000).

In terms of new shapes within the higher education landscape, for instance, as for other industries (notably automobiles, computers, mobile phones) and other areas of economic activity (fast-food and coffee-shop franchises) does the higher education industry develop ('globalize' itself) into a few mega-suppliers and global brands? Or do universities remain 'glocal'—doing much the same job globally, but doing so locally with certain national characteristics prevailing (and perhaps protected as service industries by free-trade globalization being hitherto far less evident in services than for manufactured goods)? Is there a trend towards intensely competitive institutions delivering vocational courses aimed at (hoped-for) graduate employability, and doing so reliably, flexibly, efficiently, and economically on a large scale (competing on the basis of reputation and price/fees); while others operate comfortably in the high-price, classy-brand niche (competing on the basis of prestige)?

Will higher education be subjected to 'disruptive technology'? The impact upon the traditional concept of higher education as a face-to-face activity being delivered within bricks-and-mortar campuses of ICT (information and communications technology),

MOOCs (see Chapter 3), BYOD (bring your own devices), and VLEs (virtual learning environments) all alter the 'learning analytics' of the higher education industry—introducing perhaps the AI (artificial intelligence) 'robot tutor' as a virtual (and cheap) teaching assistant. Will 'disruptive innovation' lead to the unbundling of the higher education 'product'?—the customer (student) being able to buy the teaching component alone more cheaply via remote learning, no longer forced to subsidize the university's costly research activity and its libraries, or to fund lavish sports and recreational facilities. Or will there always be a market for the idea (and ideal?) of face-to-face, small-group teaching that can't be provided on-line by some global supplier(s) dominating the digital higher education marketplace?

Moreover, might AI eliminate many graduate jobs in the coming decades, reducing the earnings incentive for 'going to uni', and negatively affecting the financial sustainability of some universities—will they shrink to educate (once again) only an elite few? Or might this potentially adverse impact of AI on graduate job opportunities mean that universities can offer new chances for re-/up-skilling, maintaining a healthy business in lifelong (re-)education? Yet, among such possible changes for the university as an entity, does the fundamental format of academic subjects and departments, of faculty hierarchy and career structures, of degree ceremonies and symbolism, remain largely unchanged? Or does the decline of 'donnish dominion' continue as the university (or most universities) become ever-more corporatist and top–down managed?

So, in short, will the university of 2050 be broadly the same as in 2000 or will it change—becoming mildly adapted or perhaps even wildly transformed? There will probably still be talk of 'the university in crisis'—but there seems always to have been, and the university adjusts, adapts, re-invents to absorb the crisis. Or this time, is the nature of the crisis really different, can there be no tinkering and tweaking of the organizational mission and format—is it time for disruptive innovation (Box 12)?

While we see a likely significant overall growth of student numbers arising from growing global demand for higher education, there will be greater segmentation and hierarchy within the global system—the pyramid of prestige within each nation's collective of universities will steepen. There will, then, be both centrifugal pressures, spreading teaching-driven higher education around the globe, with countervailing centripetal pressures pulling academic talent and financial resources to a small number of creative hubs. This will provide opportunities for the super-research universities (see Chapter 4) and the creative clusters where they are located. Less rarefied and privileged institutions will face some degree of disruptive innovation from new technologies; the elite institutions will absorb on their own terms these technologies.

Box 12. On disruptive innovation as a future for the university

Clayton Christensen and Henry Eyring, in *The Innovative University* (2011), put forward the most powerful expression of the view that higher education is (perhaps—or even probably?) on the verge of being radically transformed by 'the theory of disruptive innovation':

> universities are at a critical crossroads...the way [the university] has historically operated has become too expensive...[it] must become much more affordable, particularly by embracing online learning technology...a disruptive technology, online learning, is at work in higher education...current competitive realities indicate the need for most traditional universities to genetically reengineer themselves...changing their DNA from the inside out.

We think that the various scholars of higher education who have pointed to the longevity of the university as an organizational form as being significant are on to something: it is not an accident that so many institutions founded in the Middle Ages are still in the same business of knowledge production and transfer, when their commercial equivalents come and go over the centuries. One reason for this, we suggest, is that (as we have noted at various points in this book) the best universities (or rather key individuals within them) are constantly challenging existing knowledge, criticizing the status quo. This makes them more ready to adapt to change than most other organizations, public or private, which typically find it difficult to cope with criticism, either from within or externally. As Kerr (see Box 3) remarks: universities can change fast 'while pretending that nothing has happened'! We see no reason why this should alter. (We are amused when we see universities with experience of several hundred years of successful enterprise under wildly differing political, social, and economic conditions being lectured by management consultancies about the need for change.)

The changing nature of knowledge, and the knowledge economy, will drive the shape of higher education systems and institutional forms. The unknowability of these changes makes speculation to an extent pointless, but we believe that 'the university', broadly as we know it, will be around for a long time to come. In 2050 it will not be so very different from 2000 or even 1950, other than in scale and probably including a wider range of variants. The ever-changing university adapts, but essential components and key boundaries remain broadly intact: the concepts of intellectual autonomy and academic independence within the elite institutions; the need for a credible academic community in the successful university; the value of a careful respect for scholarship, truth, and learning in any kind of college or university wherever it may be situated within the hierarchy of institutions; the importance of a commitment to research for those universities at the apex of the pyramid of prestige, benefiting from global rankings focused on measuring research output; and the significance of academic freedom for those institutions seeking to compete via research productivity or to be successful in delivering an equally valuable and important teaching-only mission.

These reflections on knowledge and learning, have, since the 12th century, been largely focused within the organizational entity we call 'the university'—and we foresee universities, globally, continuing with this perpetual endeavour to explore and understand the human condition. But striving for that over-arching mission necessarily takes place everywhere, within a political context that directs and limits what universities can do as a result of financial, legal, social, and other constraints.

The university is a complex entity that at times appears to policy-makers as dysfunctional or even anarchic; certainly even to insiders its organization can appear mysterious. It is unavoidably messy in its structure and culture given the many and varied outcomes expected of it, and such messiness may run up against demands for transparency and accountability. In the distant past, the university was a small medieval academic guild surviving in a space between monarch and church, protected at times by each against the other. During the 19th century, in industrializing countries, it grew to become much more economically significant, not least in making itself the gatekeeper to the emerging professions that dominated 20th-century economies—and in many countries it became strongly dependent on government funding, especially for financing its enlarging research mission. Since then there has in some countries been a shift back to student fees as a significant university income-stream, along with more demands for transparency and accountability, not least from student fee-payers. The university has had to adapt to a future with new market demands, now in a marketplace: a marketplace that is local, national, and global. But in adapting and changing the university or college must remain utterly committed to its historic core values.

Further reading and references

This Further Reading section is extensive so that the reader can follow up the many themes, topics, and trends flagged in the text.

(In brackets it is indicated, where not clear from the title or the publisher, whether the book is largely about either US or UK higher education—there being little material in English about higher education in other countries beyond the OxCHEPS/Routledge comparative series referred to in the section named 'On international comparative studies of higher education systems and policy-making' and some few items listed in the section named 'On universities and colleges beyond the US and UK'.)

Introduction

Going back half a century and beyond there were quite a few more guides similar to this Very Short Introduction for a general public who then had much less direct personal experience of the university or college but who were intrigued by what went on in the Ivory Tower they financed via their taxes. There was, for instance, from 1930 item 112 in the quaint Benn's Sixpenny Library series (*The British Universities* by Charles Grant Robertson) or from 1969 in Penguin's Pelican series (British Institutions) we had *The Universities* (V.H.H. Green); and there was also James Mountford's *British Universities* (1966).

There has always been a far broader body of literature on higher education policy and on the management of the university and college in the US where mass higher education emerged as early as the 1950s. By 1980, David Riesman's *On Higher Education: The Academic Enterprise in an Era of Rising Student Consumerism* was one of some twenty-five texts in just one publisher's series on higher education—at a time when in the UK there were barely half a dozen such books: notably G.C. Moodie and R. Eustace (1974), *Power and Authority in British Universities* (Allen & Unwin).

By 2014, however, the bibliography in D. Palfreyman and T. Tapper, *Reshaping the University: The Rise of the Regulated Market in Higher Education* (Oxford University Press) runs to over 500 items drawn largely and almost equally from the burgeoning US and UK literature, exploring the continuing fierce political controversy over the commercialization and the marketization of the university and college during recent decades. On this commodification of higher education for the UK, see also A. McGettigan (2013), *The Great University Gamble: Money, Markets and the Future of Higher Education* (Pluto); and for US higher education, see D. Bok (2003), *Universities in the Marketplace: The Commercialisation of Higher Education* (Princeton University Press) along with R.L. Geiger (2004), *Knowledge and Money: Universities and the Paradox of the Marketplace* (Stanford University Press).

This debate has generated hundreds of books, many polemical and some more balanced, questioning the efficiency and effectiveness of higher education, its affordability and value-for-money. And also there are ones lamenting the fading of the public-good dimension of the university and college—for example: for the UK, see S. Collini (2012), *What Are Universities For?* (Penguin) and also his (2017) *Speaking of Universities* (Verso); from the US, see A. Delbanco (2012), *College: What It Is, Was, and Should Be* (Princeton University Press), plus L. Busch (2017), *Knowledge for Sale: The Neoliberal Takeover of Higher Education* (MIT Press); and more widely, see D. Watson (2014), *The Question of Conscience: Higher Education and Personal Responsibility* (Institute of Education Press).

On US higher education more generally, see D. Bok (2013), *Higher Education in America* (Princeton University Press); J.R. Brown and

C.M. Hoxby (2014), *How the Financial Crisis and the Great Recession Affected Higher Education* (University of Chicago Press); and D.E. Heller (2011), *The States and Public Higher Education Policy: Affordability, Access, and Accountability* (The Johns Hopkins University Press). See also the DVDs: *Ivory Tower: Is College Worth the Cost?* (Paramount, 2014) and *Starving the Beast: The Battle to Disrupt and Reform America's Public Universities* (Railyard Films, 2016).

On the history of universities and colleges

Anderson, R. (2004), *European Universities from the Enlightenment to 1914* (Oxford University Press)

Anderson, R. (2006), *British Universities Past and Present* (Hambledon Continuum)

Axtell, J. (2016), *Wisdom's Workshop: The Rise of the Modern University* (Princeton University Press)

Cobban, A. (1988), *The Medieval English Universities: Oxford and Cambridge to c1500* (Scolar Press)

Cobban, A. (1999), *University Life in the Middle Ages* (UCL Press)

Douglass, J.A. (2000), *The California Idea and American Higher Education* (Stanford University Press)

Eliot, C.W. (1908), *University Administration* (Harvard University Press) (US higher education)

Flexner, A. (1930), *Universities: American, English, German* (Oxford University Press)

Geiger, R.L. (2015), *The History of American Higher Education: Learning and Culture from the Founding to World War II* (Princeton University Press)

Karabel, J. (2005), *The Chosen: The Hidden History of Admission and Exclusion at Harvard, Yale, and Princeton* (Houghton Mifflin Company)

Lucas, C.J. (1994), *American Higher Education: A History* (St Martin's Griffin)

Malkiel, N.W. (2016), *'Keep The Damned Women Out': The Struggle for Coeducation* (Princeton University Press)

Mattingly, P.H. (2017), *American Academic Cultures: A History of Higher Education* (University of Chicago Press)

Mettler, S. (2005), *Soldiers to Citizens: The GI Bill and the Making of the Greatest Generation* (Oxford University Press)

Palfreyman, D. (2011), *London's Inns of Court* (Oracle Publishing)

Pedersen, O. (1998), *The First Universities: Studium Generale and the Origins of University Education in Europe* (Cambridge University Press)

Pratt, J. (1997), *The Polytechnic Experiment* (SRHE and Open University Press) (UK higher education)

Rashdall, H. (1895), *The Universities of Europe in the Middle Ages* (Oxford University Press; revised edition 1936)

Ridder-Symoens, H. De (ed.) (2003), *A History of the University in Europe*: Volume I, *Universities in the Middle Ages*; and Volume II, *Universities in Early Modern Europe* (Cambridge University Press)

Robbins, Lord (1980), *Higher Education Revisited* (Macmillan) (UK higher education)

Rothblat, S. (ed.) (2012), *Clark Kerr's World of Higher Education Reaches the 21st Century: Chapters in a Special History* (Springer) (US higher education—the California Master Plan)

Rudolph, F. (1990), *The American College and University: A History* (University of Georgia Press)

Rüegg, W. (ed.) (2004), *A History of the University in Europe*: Volume III, *Universities in the Nineteenth and Early Twentieth Centuries*; and Volume IV, *Universities since 1945* (Cambridge University Press)

Teixeira, P. and Dill, D.D. (2011), *Public Vices, Private Virtues?—Assessing the Effects of Marketisation in Higher Education* (Sense)

Thelin, J.R. (2011), *A History of American Higher Education* (The Johns Hopkins University Press)

Tight, M. (2009), *Higher Education in the UK since 1945* (Open University Press)

Veblen, T. (1918), *The Higher Learning in America: A Memorandum on the Conduct of Universities by Business Men* (W.B. Huebsch)

There are many histories of individual universities and colleges, including the eight volumes (running to over 7,500 pages!) of *The History of the University of Oxford* (Oxford University Press) and the four volumes of *A History of the University of Cambridge* (Cambridge University Press): some excellent examples are E. Ives et al. (2000), *The First Civic University: Birmingham, 1880–1980* (University of Birmingham Press); M. Shattock (2015), *The Impact of a University on its Environment: The University of Warwick and its Community, 1965–2015* (University of Warwick); T.G. Dyer (1985), *The University of Georgia: A Bicentennial History, 1785–1985* (University of Georgia

Press); J.W. Boyer (2015), *The University of Chicago: A History* (The University of Chicago Press); and L.W.B. Brockliss (2016) *The University of Oxford: A History* (Oxford University Press).

On international comparative studies of higher education systems and policy-making

The Routledge *International Studies in Higher Education* (series eds: D. Palfreyman, T. Tapper, and S. Thomas) in some twenty-five volumes covers worldwide comparative approaches to running university systems and determining higher education policy, and to governing individual universities and colleges. See especially: E. Hazelkorn (ed.) (2017), *Global Rankings and the Geopolitics of Higher Education: Understanding the Influence and Impact of Rankings on Higher Education, Policy and Society*; D.E. Heller and C. Callender (eds) (2013), *Student Financing of Higher Education: A Comparative Perspective*; R. Land and G. Gordon (eds) (2013), *Enhancing Quality in Higher Education*; D. Palfreyman and T. Tapper (eds) (2009), *Structuring Mass Higher Education: The Role of Elite Institutions*; D. Palfreyman et al. (eds) (2018), *Funding Higher Education: Delivering Higher Education as a Private Good*; B. Pusser et al. (eds) (2012), *Universities in the Public Sphere: Knowledge Creation and State Building in the Era of Globalisation*; P. Temple (ed.) (2012), *Universities in the Knowledge Economy: Higher Education Organisation and Global Change*; and D. Watson et al. (eds) (2011), *The Engaged University: International Perspectives on Civic Engagement*. Some of the other volumes in this series are listed later—indicated as 'ISHE'. See also for a comparative study: J. Garritzmann, *The Political Economy of Higher Education Finance: The Politics of Tuition Fees and Subsidies in OECD Countries, 1945–2015* (Palgrave Macmillan).

On working in universities and colleges

Back, L. (2016), *Academic Diary: Or Why Higher Education Still Mattters* (Goldsmiths Press) (UK higher education)

Fish, S. (2014), *Versions of Academic Freedom: From Professionalism to Revolution* (University of Chicago Press)

Gerber, L.G. (2014), *The Rise and Decline of Faculty Governance: Professionalisation and the Modern University* (The Johns Hopkins University Press)

Ginsburg, B. (2011), *The Fall of the Faculty: The Rise of the All-Administrative University and Why it Matters* (Oxford University Press) (US higher education)

Gordon, G. and Whitchurch, C. (2010, ISHE), *Academic and Professional Identities in Higher Education: The Challenges of a Diversifying Workforce* (Routledge) (UK higher education)

Halsey, A.H. (1992), *Decline of Donnish Dominion: The British Academic Profession in the Twentieth Century* (Oxford University Press)

Schumacher, J. (2017), *Doodling for Academics: A Coloring and Activity Book* (University of Chicago Press; Chicago Guides to Academic Life series)

Trowler, P. et al. (eds) (2012, ISHE), *Tribes and Territories in the C21: Rethinking the Significance of Disciplines in Higher Education* (Routledge)

Tuchman, G. (2009), *Wannabe U: Inside the Corporate University* (University of Chicago Press)

Watson, D. (2009), *The Question of Morale: Managing Happiness and Unhappiness in University Life* (Open University Press)

On applying to and studying in universities and colleges

Ainsley, R. and Smith, E. (2013), *Bluffer's Guide to University* (Bluffer's) (UK higher education)

Akers, B. and Chingos, M.M. (2016), *Game of Loans: The Rhetoric and Reality of Student Debt* (Princeton University Press) (US higher education)

Black, J. (2017), *Where am I Going and Can I have a Map? How to Take Control of your Career Plan and Make it Happen* (Robinson) (UK HE)

Blumenstyk, G. (2015), *American Higher Education in Crisis?—What Everyone Needs To Know* (Oxford University Press)

Bowen, W.G. et al. (2009), *Crossing the Finish Line: Completing College at America's Public Universities* (Princeton University Press)

Brooks, R. (2016), *Student Politics and Protest: International Perspectives* (SRHE/Routledge)

Cappelli, P. (2015), *Will College Pay Off?—A Guide to the Most Important Financial Decision You'll Ever Make* (Public Affairs) (US higher education)

Crawford, C. et al. (2016), *Family Background and University Success: Differences in Higher Education Access and Outcomes in England* (Oxford University Press)

DeSantis, A.D. (2007), *Inside Greek U: Fraternities, Sororities, and the Pursuit of Pleasure, Power, and Prestige* (University of Kentucky Press) (US higher education)

Fiske, E.B. (2016), *Fiske Guide to Colleges, 2016* (Sourcebooks) (US higher education)

Furedi, F. (2016), *What's Happened to the University? A Sociological Exploration of its Infantilisation* (Routledge) (UK higher education)

Hamilton, L.T. (2016), *Parenting to a Degree: How Family Matters for College Women's Success* (University of Chicago Press) (US higher education)

Kandiko, C.B. and Weyers, M. (2013, ISHE), *The Global Student Experience: An International and Comparative Analysis* (Routledge)

Krakauer, J. (2015), *Missolula: Rape and the Justice System in a College Town* (Knopf) (US higher education)

Lukianoff, G. (2014), *Unlearning Liberty: Campus Censorship and the End of American Debate* (Encounter Books) (US higher education)

Morris, D. (2017), *Mum's Guide to the University Search* (Book Guild Publishing) (UK higher education)

Nuwer, H. (2001), *Wrongs of Passage: Fraternities, Sororities, Hazing and Binge Drinking* (Indiana University Press) (US higher education)

Palfreyman, D. (2008), *The Oxford Tutorial* (OxCHEPS; see also the 'Papers' page of <oxcheps.new.ox.ac.uk>) (Chinese edition, 2010; Peking University Press; and Korean edition, 2018)

Rivera, L. (2015), *Pedigree: How Elite Students Get Elite Jobs* (Princeton University Press) (US higher education)

Roberts, A. (2010), *The Thinking Student's Guide to College: 75 Tips for Getting a Better Education* (University of Chicago Press) (US higher education)

Sanday, P.R. (2007), *Fraternity Gang Rape: Sex, Brotherhood, and Privilege on Campus* (New York University Press) (US higher education)

Shulman, J.L. and Bowen, W.G. (2011), *The Game of Life: College Sports and Educational Values* (Princeton University Press) (US higher education)

Selingo, J.J. (2013), *College (Un)Bound: The Future of Higher Education and What it Means for Students* (Amazon Publishing) (US higher education)

Slater, T. (2016), *Unsafe Space: The Crisis of Free Speech on Campus* (PalgraveMacmillan)

Stevens, M.L. (2007), *Creating a Class: Admissions and the Education of Elites* (Harvard University Press) (US higher education)

Tamanaha, B.Z. (2012), *Failing Law Schools* (Chicago University Press) (US higher education)

Warikoo, N.K. (2016), *The Diversity Bargain: And Other Dilemmas of Race, Admissions and Meritocracy at Elite Universities* (University of Chicago Press) (US and UK higher education)

Zimdars, A.M. (2016), *Meritocracy and the University: Selective Admissions in England and the United States* (Bloomsbury)

On teaching and learning in universities and colleges

Armstrong, E.A. and Hamilton, L.T. (2013), *Paying for the Party: How College Maintains Inequality* (Harvard University Press) (US higher education)

Arum, R. and Roksa, J. (2011), *Academically Adrift: Limited Learning on College Campuses* (University of Chicago Press) (US higher education)

Arum, R. and Roksa, J. (2014), *Aspiring Adults Adrift: Tentative Transitions of College Graduates* (University of Chicago Press) (US higher education)

Ashwin, P. et al. (2015), *Reflective Teaching in Higher Education* (Bloomsbury) (UK higher education)

Bok, D. (2006), *Our Underachieving Colleges: A Candid Look at How Much Students Learn and Why they should be Learning More* (Princeton University Press) (US higher education)

Bowen, W.G. (2013), *Higher Education in the Digital Age* (Princeton University Press) (US higher education)

Carless, D. (2015), *Excellence in University Assessment* (Routledge)

Coates, H. (2016), *The Market for Learning: Leading Transparent Higher Education* (Springer)

Hacker, A. and Dreifus, C. (2010), *Higher Education?—How Colleges Are Wasting Our Money and Failing Our Kids: And What We Can Do About It* (Times Books) (US higher education)

Kirst, M.W. and Stevens, M.L. (2015), *Remaking College: The Changing Ecology of Higher Education* (Stanford University Press) (US higher education)

Lang, J.M. (2005), *Life on the Tenure Track: Lessons from the First Year* (The Johns Hopkins University Press) (US higher education)

Lea, J. (2015), *Enhancing Learning and Teaching in Higher Education: Engaging with the Dimensions of Practice* (Open University Press) (UK higher education)

Lucas, C.J. and Murry, J.W. (2011), *New Faculty: A Practical Guide for Academic Beginners* (PalgraveMacmillan) (US higher education)

Martin, R.E. (2011), *The College Cost Disease: Higher Cost and Lower Quality* (Edward Elgar) (US higher education)

Nussbaum, M.C. (2010), *Not-for-Profit: Why Democracy Needs the Humanities* (Princeton University Press)

Small, H. (2013), *The Value of the Humanities* (Oxford University Press)

Vedder, R. (2004), *Going Broke by Degree: Why College Costs Too Much* (The AEI Press) (US higher education)

Zakaria, F. (2015), *In Defense of a Liberal Education* (W.W.Norton)

On types of university and college and on the governing, managing, and leading of universities and colleges

Angulo, A.J. (2016), *Diploma Mills: How For-profit Colleges Stiffed Students, Taxpayers, and the American Dream* (The Johns Hopkins University Press)

Barnett, R. (2011), *Being a University* (Routledge)

Bastedo, M.N. (ed.) (2013), *The Organisation of Higher Education: Managing Colleges for a New Era* (The Johns Hopkins University Press) (US higher education)

Birnbaum, R. (2000), *Management Fads in Higher Education: Where They Come From, What They Do, Why They Fail* (Jossey-Bass) (US higher education)

Bowen, W.G. (2011), *Lessons Learned: Reflections of a University President* (Princeton University Press) (US higher education)

Breneman, D.W. et al. (eds) (2006), *Earnings from Learning: The Rise of the For-Profit Universities* (State University of New York Press)

Cornford, F.M. (1908), *Microcosmographia Academica: Being a Guide for the Young Academic Politician* (Bowes & Bowes) (re Oxford and Cambridge)

Duryea, E.D. (2000), *The Academic Corporation: A History of College and University Governing Boards* (Falmer Press) (US higher education)

Ehrenberg, R.G. (2004), *Governing Academia: Who is in Charge at the Modern University?* (Cornell University Press) (US higher education)

Huisman, J. (ed.) (2009, ISHE), *International Perspectives on the Governance of Higher Education* (Routledge)

Hodgson, A. et al. (2015), *The Coming of Age for FE?—Reflections on the Past and Future Role of Further Education Colleges in England* (Institute of Education Press, UCL)

Levin, J.S. and Kater, S.T. (2017) *Understanding Community Colleges* (Routledge) (US tertiary education)

Lombardi, J.V. (2013), *How Universities Work* (The Johns Hopkins University Press)

McCaffery, P. (2010), *The Higher Education Manager's Handbook: Effective Leadership and Management in Universities and Colleges* (Routledge) (UK higher education)

Shattock, M. (2006), *Managing Good Governance in Higher Education* (Open University Press) (UK higher education)

Shattock, M. (2010), *Managing Successful Universities* (Open University Press) (UK higher education)

Shattock, M. (ed.) (2014, ISHE), *International Trends in University Governance: Autonomy, Self-government and the Distribution of Authority* (Routledge)

Stensaker, B. and Harvey, L. (eds) (2011, ISHE), *Accountability in Higher Education: Global Perspectives on Trust and Power* (Routledge)

Tapper, T. and Palfreyman, D. (2010), *The Collegial Tradition in the Age of Mass Higher Education* (Springer)

Tapper, T. and Palfreyman, D. (2011), *Oxford, the Collegiate University: Conflict, Consensus and Continuity* (Springer)

Temple, P. (2014), *The Hallmark University: Distinctiveness in Higher Education Management* (IOE Press) (UK higher education)

Tierney, W.G. and Hentschke, G.C. (2007), *New Players, Different Game: Understanding the Rise of the For-profit Colleges and Universities* (The Johns Hopkins University Press) (US higher education)

Washburn, J. (2005), *University Inc: The Corporate Corruption of Higher Education* (Basic Books) (US higher education)

Weisbrod, B.A. et al. (2008), *Mission and Money: Understanding the University* (Cambridge University Press) (US higher education)

On the physical form of the university and college, and its local impact

Birks, T. and Holford, M. (1972), *Building the New Universities* (David & Charles) (UK higher education)

Coulson, J. et al. (2015), *University Planning and Architecture* (Routledge)

Coulson, J. et al. (2015), *University Trends: Contemporary Campus Design* (Routledge)

Duke, A. (1997), *Importing Oxbridge: English Residential Colleges and American Universities* (Yale University Press)

Edwards, B. (2013), *University Architecture* (Routledge)

Florida, R. (2002), *The Rise of the Creative Class* (Basic Books)

Goddard, J. and Vallance, P. (2013), *The University and the City* (Routledge)

Muthesius, S. (2000), *The Postwar University: Utopianist Campus and College* (Yale University Press)

Shattock, M. (2015), *The Impact of a University on its Environment: The University of Warwick and its Community, 1965–2015* (University of Warwick)

Temple, P. (ed.) (2014, ISHE), *The Physical University: Contours of Space and Place in Higher Education* (Routledge)

Whyte, W. (2015), *Redbrick: A Social and Architectural History of Britain's Civic Universities* (Oxford University Press)

On the future of universities and colleges

Barnett, R. (2012, ISHE), *The Future University* (Routledge)

Caplan, B. (2017, forthcoming), *The Case against Education* (Princeton University Press)

Christiansen, C.M. and Eyring, H.J. (2011), *The Innovative University: Changing the DNA of Higher Education from the Inside Out* (Jossey-Bass)

Chow, C. and Leung, C. (2016), *Reshaping Universities for Survival in the 21st Century: New Opportunities and Paradigms* (Bentham Books)

Craig, R. (2015), *College Disrupted: The Great Unbundling of Higher Education* (St Martin's Press)

Crow, M.M. and Debars, W.B. (2015), *Designing the New American University* (The Johns Hopkins University Press)

Davis, J.A. and Farrell, M.A. (2016), *The Market Oriented University: Transforming Higher Education* (Edward Elgar)

Demillo, R.A. (2017), *Revolution in Higher Education: How a Small Band of Innovators Will Make College Accessible and Affordable* (MIT Press, paperback edition)

Douglass, J.A. (2016), *The New Flagship University* (Palgrave-Macmillan) (US higher education)

Fallis, G. (2007), *Multiversities, Ideas, and Democracy* (University of Toronto Press)

Haber, J. (2014), *MOOCs* (MIT Press)

Labaree, D.F. (2017), *A Perfect Mess: The Unlikely Ascendancy of American Higher Education* (University of Chicago Press)

Marginson, S. (2016), *The Dream is Over* (University of California Press) (US higher education—the California Master Plan)

Marginson, S. (2016), *Higher Education and the Common Good* (Melbourne University Press)

Newfield, C. (2016), *The Great Mistake: How We Wrecked Public Universities and How We Can Fix Them* (The Johns Hopkins University Press) (US higher education)

Palfreyman, D. and Tapper, T. (2014), *Reshaping the University: The Rise of the Regulated Market in Higher Education* (Oxford University Press)

Ritzen, J. (2010), *A Chance for European Universities: Or, Avoiding the Looming University Crisis in Europe* (Amsterdam University Press)

Wildavsky, B. et al. (2011), *Reinventing Higher Education: The Promise of Innovation* (Harvard Education Press) (US higher education)

Willetts, D. (2017), *A University Education* (Oxford University Press)

Zemsky, R. et al. (2005), *Remaking the American University: Market-Smart and Mission-Centred* (Rutgers University Press)

Zemsky, R. (2009), *Making Reform Work: The Case for Transforming American Higher Education* (Rutgers University Press)

Zwaan van der, B. (2017), *Higher Education in 2040: A Global Approach* (Amsterdam University Press)

On universities and colleges, and their professors, in fiction as 'the campus novel'

Amis, K. (1954), *Lucky Jim* (Penguin)

Bede, C. (1853), *The Adventures of Mr Verdant Green, An Oxford Freshman* (Nathaniel Cooke)

Beerbohm, M. (1911), *Zuleika Dobson—An Oxford Love Story* (Heinemann)

Bradbury, M. (1975), *The History Man* (Secker & Warburg)

Carter, I. (1990), *Ancient Cultures of Conceit: British University Fiction in the Post-War Years* (Routledge)

Carter, S.L. (2007), *New England White* (Random House)

Davies, A. (1986, 1988), *A Very Peculiar Practice* (Coronet); and *A Very Peculiar Practice: The New Frontier* (Methuen)

See C. Dexter for the many Inspector Morse crime novels set in Oxford colleges—the (fictional) murder rate is much higher in Oxford than in Cambridge, making the latter seem a rather dull place by comparison...

Dougill, J. (1998), *Oxford in English Literature: The Making and the Undoing of the 'English Athens'* (University of Michigan Press)

Fitzgerald, F. Scott (1920), *This Side of Paradise* (Scribner)

Galbraith, J.K. (1990), *The Tenured Professor* (Houghton Mifflin)

Hynes, J. (2001), *The Lecturer's Tale* (Picador)

Jarrell, R. (1952), *Pictures from an Institution* (University of Chicago Press)

Lodge, D. (1975), *Changing Places*; (1984), *Small World*; and (1989), *Nice Work* (all Vintage; also published by Penguin)

Lurie, A. (1974), *The War Between the Tates* (Random House)

McCarthy, M. (1951), *The Groves of Academe* (Harcourt)

Proctor, M.R. (1957), *The English University Novel* (University of California Press)

Sayers, D.L. (1935), *Gaudy Night* (Victor Gollancz)

Sharpe, T. (1976), *Porterhouse Blue* (Arrow Books)

Showalter, E. (2005), *Faculty Towers: The Academic Novel and its Discontents* (Oxford University Press)

Snow, C.P. (1951), *The Masters* (MacMillan)

Waugh, E. (1945), *Brideshead Revisited* (Chapman & Hall)

Wolfe, T. (2004), *I Am Charlotte Simmons* (Picador)

On universities and colleges beyond the US and UK

See also the items marked 'ISHE' and as listed in the section named 'On international comparative studies of higher education systems and policy-making', for coverage of higher education across many nations

Agarwal, P. (2009), *Indian Higher Education: Envisioning the Future* (Sage)

Altbach, P.G. and Umakoshi, T. (2004), *Asian Universities: Historical Perspectives and Contemporary Challenges* (The Johns Hopkins University Press)

Altbach, P.G. and Balan, J. (2007), *World-Class Worldwide: Transforming Research Universities in Asia and Latin America* (The Johns Hopkins University Press)

Altbach, P.G. (2016), *Global Perspectives on Higher Education* (The Johns Hopkins University Press)

Côté, J.E. and Allahar, A.L. (2007), *Ivory Tower Blues: A University System in Crisis* (University of Toronto Press)

Datta, S. (2017), *A History of the Indian University System: Emerging from the Shadows of the Past* (PalgraveMacmillan)

Kühl, S. (2014), *The Sudoku Effect: Universities in the Vicious Circle of Bureaucracy* (Springer) (re European universities and the Bologna Process)

Marginson, S. et al. (eds) (2010), *Higher Education in the Asia-Pacific: Strategic Responses to Globalisation* (Springer)

Rhoads, R.A. et al. (2014), *China's Rising Research Universities: A New Era of Global Ambition* (The Johns Hopkins University Press)

Salmi, J. (2009), *The Challenge of Establishing World-Class Universities* (The World Bank)

On the legal framework within which US and UK universities and colleges operate

Farrington, D. and Palfreyman, D. (2012), *The Law of Higher Education* (Oxford University Press) (UK higher education)

Kaplin, W.A. and Lee, B.A. (2013), *The Law of Higher Education* (Jossey-Bass) (US higher education)

Box references

Box 2. H. Rashdall (1895), *The Universities of Europe in the Middle Ages* (Oxford University Press; revised edn: F.M. Powicke and A.B. Emden (eds) (1936), Oxford University Press)

Box 3. C. Kerr (1963), *The Uses of the University* (Harvard University Press)

Box 4. John Henry, Cardinal Newman (1852), *The Idea of a University* (Longmans)

Box 5. A. Davies (1986), *A Very Peculiar Practice* (Coronet); and M. Bradbury (1975), *The History Man* (Secker & Warburg)

Box 6. C.P. Snow (1951), *The Masters* (MacMillan)

Box 7. F.M. Cornford (1908), *Microcosmographia Academica: Being a Guide for the Young Academic Politician* (Bowes & Bowes); and C.W. Eliot (1908), *University Administration* (Houghton Mifflin Company)

Box 8. T. Wolfe (2004), *I am Charlotte Simmons* (Picador); O. Johnson (1912), *Stover at Yale* (Little, Brown, and Company); F. Scott Fitzgerald (1920), *This Side of Paradise* (Scribner); J.P. Marquand (1937), *The Late George Apley* (Little, Brown, and Company); E. Waugh (1945), *Brideshead Revisited* (Chapman & Hall)

Box 9. M. Bradbury (1975), *The History Man* (Secker & Warburg)

Box 10. D. Farrington and D. Palfreyman (2012), *The Law of Higher Education* (Oxford University Press) (UK higher education); and W.A. Kaplin and B.A. Lee (2013), *The Law of Higher Education* (Jossey-Bass) (US higher education)

Box 11. K. Amis (1954), *Lucky Jim* (Penguin); B. Truscot (1943), *Red Brick University* (Faber & Faber); M. Innes (1936), *Death at the President's Lodgings* (Penguin edition, 1988); J.I.M. Stewart (1974–8: five novels in the series), *A Staircase in Surrey* (Victor Gollancz)

Box 12. C.M. Christensen and H.J. Eyring (2011), *The Innovative University: Changing the DNA of Higher Education from the Inside Out* (Jossey-Bass)

Index

SOCIAL MEDIA
Very Short Introduction

Join our community
www.oup.com/vsi

- Join us online at the official Very Short Introductions **Facebook** page.
- Access the thoughts and musings of our authors with our online **blog**.
- Sign up for our monthly **e-newsletter** to receive information on all new titles publishing that month.
- Browse the full range of Very Short Introductions online.
- Read **extracts** from the Introductions for free.
- If you are a teacher or lecturer you can order inspection copies quickly and simply via our website.

ONLINE CATALOGUE
A Very Short Introduction

Our online catalogue is designed to make it easy to find your ideal Very Short Introduction. View the entire collection by subject area, watch author videos, read sample chapters, and download reading guides.

http://global.oup.com/uk/academic/general/vsi_list/